2012

D0276627

THROUGH
ALBERT'S EYES

VOLUME 2 OF *THE BRITISH NAVY AT WAR AND PEACE*

A. BENTLEY-BUCKLE

SERIES EDITOR: CAPTAIN PETER HORE

Whittles Publishing

Published by
Whittles Publishing Ltd.,
Dunbeath,
Caithness, KW6 6EG,
Scotland, UK

www.whittlespublishing.com

ISBN 978-184995-066-4

THE BRITISH NAVY AT WAR AND PEACE

Series editor: Captain P. G. Hore FRHistS CMIL RN rtd

Volume 1 *Wingfield at War* M. Wingfield
ISBN 978-184995-064-0

Printed in the UK by Ashford Colour Press Ltd, Gosport, Hampshire

Contents

John Worsley's image of Tony Bentley-Buckle, 1921–2010

FOREWORD

Tony Bentley-Buckle was a child of empire, brought up at boarding school and in the care of elderly and peripatetic aunts. Today this might be consider as disadvantageous, but Tony's life was full of adventure and entrepreneurism on a grand scale, and he fitted more into his war and his life than many another man. In the first Elizabethan age he would have ranked with the greats and laid the foundations of empire, instead of witnessing its decline.

Having joined the Royal Navy before the war, he found himself on the Northern Patrol (the blockade of Germany) and as a teenager in command of captured ships. For bringing a ship through the minefields into Scapa Flow, young Midshipman Bentley-Buckle was interviewed by the famously ferocious Admiral Max Horton, who recommended him for advanced promotion.

After witnessing some of the opening moves of the war, Bentley-Buckle volunteered in a fit of derring-do for 'special service', without knowing what this meant, and found himself under training for one of Britain's secret navies. As a beach commando, he was one of the first ashore at the Allied landings on Sicily and one of the first Allied officers to cross the Strait of Messina. On Reggio beach he survived to tell the tale of how he was one of the few people to order General Montgomery to stop talking and not to block the exit of the beach.

Soon Bentley-Buckle was seconded even deeper into British secret services when he was lent to MI9, the escape and evasion agency, and he helped rescue hundreds of British prisoners of war who had been in Italian hands. By schoolboy trick he also captured a German despatch-rider with his motorbike and his messages.

Next he mounted a forward operating base on an island in the Adriatic and fought against crack German troops before being taken prisoner himself. He escaped, was recaptured and badly beaten and eventually reached a prisoner-of-war camp known as Marlag und Milag Nord and occupied by men of the British Merchant Navy and Royal Navy, located around the village of Westertimke, around 19 miles north-east of Bremen. There he took part in one of the most audacious escapes of the war – and certainly the cheekiest – his part being to make the moving eyes of the dummy known as 'Albert RN'. He survived a death march and eventually thumbed a lift home in a Dakota, to arrive unannounced in England.

After the war he learnt to fly, intending to join the Fleet Air Arm, but, still a young man, he decided instead to set out on a new adventure, sailing via the Mediterranean to East Africa, where he started salvage work and founded a shipping company. Needing to visit his expanding business interests, he bought an aeroplane, in which he flew between Europe and Africa, and he represented Kenya, his adopted country, at the 1960 Olympics. Tony found himself a player on the international stage, dealing with bishops, governments and fossil-fish, and meeting with several triumphs and disasters, treating, like a true son of empire, those two impostors just the same.

At the end of his exploits Tony lived happily in retirement in Beaulieu, but by 2005 he was diagnosed with glaucoma and had to give up driving. In 2007 he showed signs of dementia, though he continued to travel to South Africa until April 2010. His finished his long and eventful career at Woodpeckers, a very pleasant nursing home in Brockenhurst in the New Forest, and died peacefully in his sleep during the night of 23/24 May 2010.

Tony's life, in which he treated each new turn and challenge as a problem waiting to be solved, will be an inspiration to anyone who reads this, his modestly told autobiography.

David Balme
Lymington

1

CHILD OF EMPIRE

I was born on 13 August 1921 in a luxurious bedroom at the Palace Hotel on the seafront in Knokke, Belgium. My father, Noel William, known as Box (having been born on Boxing Day), was a rubber planter in Ceylon and on holiday in Belgium with my mother Mary at the time. They had married in Ceylon in 1916. Although christened Anthony, I was known as Tony and was taken back to the rubber estate at Jambulande Maskeliya, where I stayed until the age of five. I was a shy little boy with fair curly hair and when I was three my father considered it was time for the baby curls to go and called the Sinhalese barber to the house. When my mother saw what had happened to my hair she was furious.

The family returned to England by sea in 1926 and about this time my father bought a flat in Monte Carlo with the idea of retiring. Unfortunately all his money was in rubber shares which, when the flat was bought, stood at over 15 shillings (75p) a share. Due to the discovery of synthetic rubber and the worldwide slump in the late twenties, rubber shares dropped to

Box and Mary's wedding, Ceylon

[Above right] *Tony Bentley-Buckle aged six with an early ship*

[Above left] *Tony Bentley-Buckle aged seven*

Tony Bentley-Buckle on the beach, Knokke, Belgium

less than a penny. As a result the flat in Monte Carlo was sold together with the large Austin car, the chauffeur was no longer required, and my parents returned to Ceylon to start all over again.

In 1926 my sister Pat and I were left in England with two of our mother's sisters, Aunts Hilda and Agnes Rankin in a house named Bramber, in Aldenham Avenue, Radlett, Hertfordshire. Pat was four and a half years older than I and taken under Aunt Hilda's wing. Aunt Agnes did likewise with me. It was a strict Victorian existence, with Pat and me living mainly in the upstairs nursery and only allowed downstairs for tea in the afternoon, when crumpets were a real treat. We sat in the dining room for lunch and Pat was apt to slouch over the table and had to wear a back support. If anything was left on the plate it was served at the next meal. After lunch I was forced to lie down for a rest and

Tony, Mary, Box and Pat

forbidden to get up until told rest time was over. Our upbringing was extremely strict but I doubt if Agnes knew anything about the facts of life up to her dying day. Throughout our time with them the facts of life were never mentioned and as I grew up I still believed that a baby was brought by a stork and deposited down the chimney. Occasionally I had an itching backside which was obviously worms. I called it 'tail tickling' and Agnes used to rub a little ointment on the place where it itched. Another time I went into Pat's bedroom when she was completely naked, and I was hauled out by Agnes and given a good smacking. The lesson is that children should not be brought up by maiden aunts.

I remember at my prep school during tea one day I said to the other boys at my table that I would love to see a baby born. Several of the other boys said 'That's a dirty thing', and that was the end of the conversation, leaving me more worried about the whole process.

My first glimmer of the facts of life was just before I left Ampleforth in July 1939. The headmaster, Father Paul Neville, called me into his study and said, 'Now that you are going into the wide world there are certain things you should be warned about: that is the danger of women.' He said he knew of occasions when girls had enticed boys into their bedrooms and they had slept together, sometimes with dire consequences.

3

Aunts Hilda [left] and Agnes [right] with Tony [centre]

The true facts of life were only learnt by asking other people. Quite often on our walks with Aunt Agnes I would ask her about birds with eggs in their nests that eventually hatched and produced other little birds. Agnes could quite well have elaborated on how they arrived in the nest but I wonder today whether she knew anything about it. I now consider it wrong for young children to be brought up by maiden aunts who are very religious and know little about the facts of life themselves.

Pat went to St Mary's Convent in Ascot. I have a vivid recollection of our mother arriving from Ceylon at our aunts' house to see Pat at the end of lunch one day. Pat came out from the dining room and rushed to our mother with rice pudding dropping out of her bloomers, this being the place to hide something she did not like to eat! The aunts had very little money to spend on us and our parents had very little to contribute. In 1928 the aunts took us first to Lausanne in Switzerland and later to Clarens, near Montreux, where we went to Villa Dubochet, a day school on the banks of Lake Geneva. I was still very shy, especially as my nose had assumed an embarrassing size. To my way of thinking, I could not join the other pupils in the dining room and instead was placed on my own in a little room nearby.

After at least a year at Clarens the aunts took Pat and me by train to Knokke in Belgium, where we lived for a number of years in various flats. Then Pat was sent to the English Convent of Bruges and I went to a day school next to the golf course. To my great embarrassment,

I was dressed like Little Lord Fauntleroy in frilly shirts and corduroy trousers. Amongst the other pupils I was soon given the name of 'Auntie'. I so hated the school and the teasing from the other children that I ran away and found my way to the flat we were then occupying in Le Zoute. The aunts did not take kindly to my desertion and I was forced to return to the school. Happily, my mother returned on leave from Ceylon and was horrified to see my clothing. She immediately took me shopping for grey flannel shorts and a normal shirt, but the damage had been done and I flatly refused to go back to that school.

My mother was very understanding and in 1930 took me to St Richard's, a boarding school in Little Malvern, England that catered for boys up to public school entry. Life at St Richard's was very happy. I had pocket money each term of 2s. 6d.[1] and remained there as a boarder for the rest of my prep school days, taking holidays with the aunts in Knokke. Aunt Agnes used to come to England with me as it was deemed far too dangerous for me to travel on my own. We caught the ferry to Ostend, where she sat in a leopardskin fur coat on deck, occasionally, in bad weather, rushing off to be sick. Life progressed in Belgium and eventually I was allowed a small bicycle, which I polished and looked after myself. My mother, whom I loved dearly, used to come back from Ceylon from time to time, but my father was still not sufficiently wealthy to accompany her.

The great day came for public school and I passed Common Entrance for Ampleforth in July 1930. I was in St Bede's House in the main building with, for the young boys, a dormitory with cubicles on the top floor. My main hobby there was to take a small piece of cheese over which I suspended a straight heavy sharpened wire with a band on, with the object of ending the life of a rat which used to wander around. Regrettably, I was unsuccessful, having only one near miss to my credit. If rats were caught the housemaster gave sixpence (2½ pence) for each tail. A friend in another house owned a ferret that he often kept in his pocket. One day he mentioned that down in the valley by the sewage plant there were copious numbers of rats. Armed with his ferret we used to go down to the sewage plant and became quite good rat-catchers, keeping my housemaster liberally supplied with rats' tails. As my fortune grew his suspicions increased to the point where, after another delivery of rats' tails, I was asked from where they came. On telling the truth, I was told that the sewage farm was thereafter out of bounds and that was the end of the sixpences. My friend and I shared the booty, with the bigger share going to my friend as owner of the ferret.

Sometimes in class my attention would lapse and I used to flex the muscles in my arm to another pupil. If I was caught the master would say, 'Go and see your housemaster tonight before going to bed.' I used to knock on his door and say, 'Excuse me, sir, but I was told to come and see you for fooling in class.' He would reply 'Not again' and go to a drawer in his study and take out a ferule of flattened whalebone. I put out one hand and he would hit it with the whalebone, which was extremely painful, and then the other was likewise hit. If the housemaster thought I deserved any more discipline, the process was repeated, and my hands were severely bruised on occasions. When I went into the sixth form in July 1938, having taken School Certificate and passed reasonably well, I was allotted a room of my own where, apart from the bed, there was a homemade armchair. As the end of my schooldays approached, there was family concern as to what I would do in life, and I opted to join the Royal Navy.

Tony aged 16

In the summer holidays of 1938 before the last term, my parents sent the money for my return passage to Ceylon. By this time the aunts had temporarily abandoned Knokke and lived in a small flat on the outskirts of Guildford. The next-door neighbours were the Weatherills, who had two daughters and a son, Jack. He was at school in Malvern and came with me to Ceylon. The stay was a mere three weeks as the only way to get there was by

6

sea. We took the train to Marseilles where we joined the Bibby Line ship *Derbyshire*. The Bibby Line ships sailed from Ceylon to India, where the small amount of cargo on board was discharged, and then returned to England. The holiday in Ceylon was a great treat, but sadly was the last time I saw my mother. Early in the next term, in August 1938, Aunt Agnes, accompanied by Mrs Weatherill, arrived at the school to take me out. During the drive Agnes said, 'Your mother is very ill.' I turned to her and said, 'She's dead.' Two days earlier, during lunch at St Bede's top table, where the housemaster presided, I had suddenly looked up and said to a boy near me, 'My mother's dead.' The housemaster said, 'How dare you say such a thing?' and I replied, 'I am sorry, my mother's dead.' My mother had suffered a heart attack and died aged fifty-two in the dentist's chair in Colombo at the same moment as the housemaster reprimanded me. We had a very close relationship and somehow my sixth sense told me of her death, which had occurred due to an overdose of gas.

2

DOWN TO THE SEA IN SHIPS

I n late 1938 I sat the examination for the Navy and luckily passed out as 33rd of that term in the Executive branch. I was kitted out with a cadet's uniform by Gieves of Piccadilly, and on 1 January 1939 walked down the gangway of the training ship HMS *Frobisher* in Portsmouth.[2] The ship had been laid up for training duties in Fareham Creek. Training was very rigid, with various courses, the Admiralty endeavouring to instil seamanship into the young gentlemen, as we were called. When queuing up for our first pay packet, I was in front of

Cadet Bentley-Buckle

a cadet named David Borthwick. We went our separate ways and met again forty-five years later as neighbours in Beaulieu, Hampshire.

At the conclusion of the first term all cadets left the *Frobisher* and after three weeks' leave I joined, on 2 May 1939, HMS *Vindictive*, a similar-type seagoing cruiser, for cruises, the first of which was to Brest in France, then La Baule, near St-Nazaire.[3] I have a vivid recollection of going ashore with a couple of friends to a local hotel where we had *poulet au riz*, which was the finest chicken dish I had ever tasted.

From La Baule we continued to Iceland where about a day out I suffered my one and only bout of seasickness. The cadets all placed their caps on the deck by the mess table and regrettably a bottle of piccalilli, minus lid, slid down the table, landing squarely in my cap as the ship rolled in a somewhat confused sea. It was too much for me. I nipped out on deck to the rail and gave the sea most of my lunch! Reykjavik was, to young sailors, a wonderful stop. Fishing over the side with a line having several hooks meant we invariably came up with fish equal to the number of hooks. On going ashore we were joined by all the nubile young ladies of the town, amongst whom were some very pretty girls, and we occasionally cavorted in the public swimming baths, heated by the natural hot geysers, abundant throughout the island. After the cruise we earned four weeks' leave before a final cruise prior to being posted to a seagoing ship. In pre-war days the cadets had a certain choice as to the area where they served. There was the Home Fleet, Mediterranean Fleet, Eastern Fleet and the West Indies station.

In early August 1939 I went on holiday to visit the aunts, who had resumed living in Knokke, and within three weeks a telegram arrived ordering me to return immediately and report to the Admiralty. Chamberlain had just returned from Munich waving a slip of paper and proclaiming 'Peace in our time', but obviously this was not reciprocated by the Admiralty.[4] After a tearful goodbye from the aunts, who said, 'Do be careful', I took the ferry from Ostend, and reported to the Admiralty in London on 26 August 1939, where I was given a rail warrant to proceed with all my gear to Scapa Flow via Rosyth to join HMS *Dunedin* as a cadet.[5] Whilst there, the commander-in-chief Rosyth, a full admiral, cleared lower decks, which meant everyone assembled. The commander-in-chief, accompanied by the chief of staff, addressed us, saying, 'Gentlemen, there is a conflict about to engulf us all which very few of us here will survive.'[6]

At that moment a signalman appeared, interrupting proceedings. He passed a signal to the chief of staff, who glanced at it and placed it in his pocket. This was too much for the commander-in-chief,

HMS Dunedin

who was by then in full flow. He said, 'Come on, chief of staff, read it out.' Having just told the group in his address that maybe at that very moment hundreds upon hundreds of German aircraft might be descending on the island, he must have believed this would add spice to his oratory. I should add that at this time a number of trawlers had been taken over by the Admiralty and fitted with boom defence nets for sealing harbour entrances. The chief of staff sheepishly produced the signal and read, 'Commander-in-Chief Rosyth. From *Gracie Fields*. Am making water fast.' This of course was one of the trawlers taken over by the Admiralty. The great mirth caused by this reading brought an abrupt end to the commander-in-chief's speech.

Whilst at Rosyth I met four other young cadets, all likewise going to HMS *Dunedin*. We proceeded in very cold, third-class carriages that terminated at the Pentland Firth, where we caught a small Admiralty ferry across to Scapa Flow and the various vessels to which we had all been appointed. The ship was not quite what I had expected. The *Dunedin* was an old D-class cruiser built in 1915; other ships in the class were *Diomede*, *Despatch*, *Durban* and *Delhi*. After the removal of her topmast the *Dunedin* was installed with the first experimental radar equipment. The gunroom was rather cramped and used as a dining mess and sitting room. The sleeping area was in an alleyway outside where hammocks were slung, and by this time it was the opinion that sleeping in a hammock was far more comfortable than a bed. On each side of the upper deck amidships were two sets of torpedo tubes which were fore and aft whilst in harbour and swivelled outboard whilst the ship was at sea, leaving a gap in the rails of about 6 feet.

Once everyone had settled in, the ship put to sea on 1 September 1939 and patrolled between Scapa Flow and the Faroe Islands. Two days later war was declared and a regulation came into force at sea that no ship could stop for fear of German U-boat attack. On our first patrol, whilst the torpedo tubes were swivelled outboard thereby leaving a gap in the guard rails, I witnessed to my horror an able seaman slip on the deck with the roll of the ship and disappear over the side. The man surfaced and waved his arms, shouting for help. I rushed to the bridge and shouted to the officer of the watch, 'Man overboard!' However, thanks to the new regulations, the ship was obliged to sail on and the able seaman was lost. The captain was a delightful man named Charles Lambe who had been an equerry at the Palace.[7] The commander under him was an old dead-beat who had been retired and recalled for the war. He was a most unpleasant, corpulent man who had no time for midshipmen let alone us cadets.

On the declaration of war on 3 September 1939, our ship was patrolling an area of the North Sea, first between Scapa Flow and the Faroe Islands and later during the winter of 1939 between the Faroes and Iceland. The sea was generally extremely rough and the weather very cold, so much so that on numerous occasions the guard rails and forward gun mountings were covered in ice. The commander felt it would be good training for the cadets to accompany the sailors on to the fo'c'sle to chip off the ice from the rails and gun mountings, which could not be trained due to the ice. On one occasion, having overslept our time off in our hammocks, orders were given to the cadets by the commander to climb the shortened main mast and stay there until ordered down. The wind was so bitter that when the cadets were told to come down they were too cold to use their arms, and had to be lowered by rope. The watches were four hours on and four hours off throughout the patrols and we slept, hot-bunking, in hammocks when below. When on watch we had to partially lash-up a hammock in case of a disaster, as it acted, for a short period, as a lifebelt.

On the second patrol a German submarine, *U-47*, penetrated the boom defence nets and torpedoed the battleship *Royal Oak*, which suffered considerable loss of life. The U-boat returned to Germany where the commander, Günther Prien, was awarded the Iron Cross by Adolf Hitler. From October onwards, the ship instead of returning to Scapa Flow berthed in Sullom Voe in the Shetlands, a long narrow inlet. There was very little to do except walk on the moors. On one occasion three of us set off across the moors with a .410 shotgun in search of rabbits. There were none to be had and we eventually ended up at a crofter's cottage and asked if we could buy some tea. The wife took us in and gave us a first-class tea with angel cake. When we tried to pay, she at first refused point blank. However, when pressed, she asked could we afford to pay her three pence?

As the nights lengthened and the further north we patrolled, the crew were occasionally treated to the aurora borealis. The streaks lighting up the sky were a magnificent sight. The patrols were to stop and search any shipping that appeared over the horizon, examining its manifest and destination. If there was any doubt, the boarding party, which generally comprised one officer, a petty officer and at least two seamen, would remain on board and accompany the ship into Kirkwall for further examination. On one patrol, after ten days at sea, the boarding parties had remained on board to escort several ships into Scapa.

The captain turned to me while on watch on the bridge and said, 'Young Buckle, there are too many officers away from the ship and when the next ship is sighted you are to be the boarding officer.'

This was most exciting for me and, lo and behold, the next day over the horizon came a small Swedish cargo vessel, which I boarded, and it was deemed after examination of the manifest that it should proceed into Kirkwall. I had been given the necessary Admiralty chart from the *Dunedin* showing the area of minefields and the swept channel that had to be scrupulously followed. This was too much for the old Swedish captain, who shook his shoulders, proceeded to his cabin with a bottle of port and refused to be responsible for the navigation of his ship. The Fair Island channel down which it was necessary to proceed was well charted, and I found no trouble in taking the ship, with the help of its chief officer, safely into Kirkwall. The procedure was for the boarding officer to report ashore and then wait for the *Dunedin* to return to Scapa at the end of its patrol.

The commander-in-chief, Northern Patrol, was Admiral Max Horton, by whom I was interrogated and asked how I had proceeded into Kirkwall.[8] I pointed out the swept Fair Island channel, and on seeing from my uniform that I was still a cadet, it appeared to the admiral that I had shown ability beyond my present training. The admiral kindly wrote to the Admiralty proposing that I be given accelerated promotion. Shortly afterwards I received a letter from the Admiralty giving me two months' accelerated promotion, which came in very handy when I became a midshipman and my pay increased

Cadet A.W.Bentley Buckle.H.M.S.Dunedin.

From   The Vice Admiral Commanding. Northern Patrol.

Date .14th November.1939.

To   The Secretary of the Admirality.

The Commandere Commanding,11th Cruiser Squadron.

The Commanding Officer H.M.S.Dunedin.

(Copy to :- Commander in Chief,Home Fleet.)

I wish to bring to the favourable notice of Their Lordships the achievement of Cadet A.W.Bentley Buckle of H.M.S.Dunedin when sent as Officer-in-Charge of Armed Guard on board the Swedish Ship,Pedro Christopherson,gross tonnage 3,767 on 9th October 1939.

2.The Master was so frightened of mines and submarines in the Fair Island Channel that he retired to his cabin with a bottle of Port and cried. Cadet Buckle then took charge of the ship and brought her safely to port.

3. In view of the qualities displayed by Cadet Buckle I submit that he may be considered for accelerated promotion.

Signed   Max Horton.

Vice Admiral.

Max Horton's letter recommending young Bentley-Buckle for accelerated promotion from the one shilling a day (5p) earned by cadets to the then liveable amount of five shillings a day for midshipmen.

A further opportunity occurred for me when I was again told by Captain Lambe that I would be the next boarding officer, to see the Swedish American Line passenger ship *Drottningholm* appear.[9] I had by this time become the owner of a new issue duffle coat and a pair of sea boots. These I donned and was rowed over by a cutter's crew to a rope ladder dangling from the boat deck of the *Drottningholm*. This I mounted for an ascent that seemed to continue for a very long time and I eventually landed on the boat deck amongst a crowd of blanketed and cold passengers.

I stuck out what little chest I had and put on my cap at a jaunty angle, only to hear a strident female American voice saying, 'Gee, honey, isn't it a crime to send kids to war?' I left the deck pretty smartly.

Around Christmas 1939 the *Dunedin* had taken such a battering on patrol that few of the guns would train, and the ship proceeded to Govan for repairs. Three cadets, including myself, decided to pool our money and have dinner ashore at the best hotel, the Station Hotel in Glasgow. To our embarrassment, two tables away were the captain and the commander who nodded to us, and towards the end of our meal we emptied our pockets and worked out whether we had sufficient money to pay. We then summoned the waiter and said, 'The bill, please.' The waiter replied, 'It is all right, young gentlemen – the captain over there has paid for your dinner.' This was typical of Charles Lambe.

After a few days' leave, during which I stayed with an uncle, Richard Rankin, at Neston outside Liverpool, I arranged to purchase a short-wave radio receiver that we could have in the gunroom. I remember the cost was £31 and my uncle generously paid half this amount. When I returned to the ship after leave with our new toy, the rest of the cadets in the gunroom were not amused and decided they did not have enough money to pay the remaining £15. Later they relented and we all clubbed together and sent the payment to my uncle.

At the end of the refit *Dunedin* proceeded to sea and after a couple of days going west the captain announced that we were bound for

Bermuda off the American coast. The whole ship's company thereafter had a completely different attitude and counted the days until arrival. Unfortunately, three days out from Bermuda the ship ran into an appalling storm, and had to heave to at the slowest speed possible to keep steerageway. To get from the gunroom to the bridge it was necessary to climb a metal ladder on to a walkway, which went a third of the way up the funnels. I happened to be on watch when the storm became so bad that no one could leave the bridge or get back aft again due to the sea breaking over the ship. However, Bermuda was reached in good form and I remember that on entering Bermuda the ship proceeded inside the reef through a channel up to the dockyard. On the edge of the reef was a very elegant passenger ship that lay abandoned, having gone aground one night. We young midshipmen had a marvellous time in Bermuda and inevitably met many Bermudan girls. I was particularly attracted to a blonde girl, Betty Butterfield, who happily reciprocated, perhaps with less intensity than me. Sadly, I did not realise that her father owned the Butterfield Bank.

The *Dunedin* underwent a major refit in the dockyard: the decks were recaulked and the gun mountings overhauled, all of which took several months. Amongst the ship's boats was a small fast launch, called a skimmer. It had a little cuddy aft and the driver sat forward. Charles

Émile Bertin

15

Lambe, who was thirty-nine at that time, had managed to get his girlfriend (an extremely attractive lady), over to Bermuda and leased a small beach house in one of the many coves. He suggested I should be trained as the main driver of the skimmer. This entailed driving Charles Lambe to the cove of his girlfriend's house at the end of the day and collecting him again in the morning. On the first delivery he said to me, 'I am sure you have enough discretion to keep my movements confidential!'

After the refit the ship went on patrol, and lay off the island of Martinique. A couple of days later two French warships arrived, the *Émile Bertin*, a new fast French cruiser, and an older aircraft carrier, the *Béarn*. Charles Lambe summoned me with instructions to take another midshipman and the skimmer quietly into the harbour each night after dark, pick up a buoy and watch the *Émile Bertin*. The instructions were that if the ship was seen to shorten in her lines or proceed to sea I had to return as quickly as possible and report. This charade went on for nearly three weeks, after which we proceeded to St Lucia. During one of our patrols of the Mona Passage between Haiti and Santa Domingo we intercepted the *Heidelberg*, a German ship flying a Dutch flag. Having broken out of Aruba in an attempt to make it across the Atlantic and home, *Heidelberg* was intercepted by *Dunedin* at around 7.30 a.m. on 2 March. The crew of the *Heidelberg* began scuttling her before *Dunedin* could put a boarding party in place, setting fire to the ship, and then taking to the lifeboats. *Dunedin* picked up around twenty-five of them (mostly boys) and then fired several 6-inch shells into her. She burned for hours, finally sinking at around 5.00 p.m. The prisoners were eventually landed in Jamaica. On another occasion we intercepted the German ship *Hannover* full of cargo. Although the crew attempted to scuttle her, some of the cargo had shifted and partially blocked the propeller shaft casing where the crew had tried to sink the ship. We towed her to Jamaica.

Some years after the war I read an interesting book written by a Canadian, entitled *A Man Called Intrepid*.[10] He was deeply involved in intelligence with the British government. In the book it came to light that the *Émile Bertin* had arrived in Martinique with a huge quantity of French gold bullion. The British government was concerned that she might go further south to South America and use the gold for the purchase of supplies for the Vichy French and help Germany. Whether this was true, history does not relate.[11]

Dunedin returned to Portsmouth around July 1940 during a period of considerable German aerial activity where they frequently came over at night to bomb the harbour, thankfully always being driven off by the RAF. This was the time of the Battle of Britain and, sadly, time for Charles Lambe to leave the *Dunedin*. He was later promoted to admiral of the fleet and died in 1960. All the midshipmen left *Dunedin* in September 1940 to do further training, starting with a torpedo course at Roedean Girls' School near Brighton, which had been evacuated, and afterwards a gunnery course at HMS *Excellent*, on Whale Island, Portsmouth. We then attended a navigation course held during the day at HMS *Dryad*, but as the accommodation was badly damaged by German bombs we moved to Southwick House. This was owned by an old man named Thistlethwaite, who I remember one evening appeared in a nightgown at the top of the stairs holding a candlestick.[12]

After our courses we were all again appointed to seagoing ships and I arrived aboard HMS *Edinburgh* at Rosyth. She and her sister-ship *Belfast* were brand-new heavy cruisers of 13,500 tons that had both been mined off the Norwegian coast and returned to Rosyth for repair. Our greatest asset on board was the dental lieutenant known as Toothy Thexton, who could play almost any instrument handed to him. Invariably when the ship put into Scapa Flow or any other port, Toothy would hoist the gin pennant as a signal to other nearby ships that there would be a concert.

The *Edinburgh* patrolled from Scapa Flow up to the Faroe Islands and Iceland and on one patrol off the Faroes we sighted a German weather trawler, which was boarded and the Enigma codebooks captured.[13] This was about the time the U-boat *U-110* was depth-charged and blown to the surface by a corvette, HMS *Bulldog*. David Balme, then a young sub lieutenant, was sent over in a whaler to board the submarine, whose crew was then abandoning ship. The crew were picked up, and David with his artificers descended into the submarine and discovered a complete Enigma machine with the codebooks in the captain's cabin.

During the winter *Edinburgh* was involved in Russian convoys as far as Murmansk, which was again bitterly cold. After the Faroes patrol, the *Edinburgh* sailed to Freetown in West Africa, which was a relaxing change from our previous tour. Housed in a hangar amidships was a Supermarine Walrus seaplane. Its main use was to patrol for other vessels, but it was slow and cumbersome with a limited range. While at Freetown the Walrus was wheeled out of the hangar and hitched to a catapult on the flight deck to inspect the river. The pilot sat on the left of the cockpit with the co-pilot and navigator on his right with enough room for a third passenger, myself, behind the pilot. This was my first experience of flying. After the cockpit check had been carried out, the controls were set for straight and level flight and the pilot raised his hand. This was the signal to the other members of the crew to brace, and to the catapult operator on deck that he was ready. The pilot would then lower his arm, grab hold of the stick and the catapult operator would operate the catapult. The aircraft quickly gathered speed and lumbered into the skies, hopefully in a straight line. We had a very pleasant afternoon's run up the river with in-flight sandwiches. When returning to the ship the drill was to fly over the vessel which would then alter course until there was a flat lee on one side. The Walrus would then land in the lee and taxi fairly close to the ship's side, enabling a hook to be attached and the aircraft lifted on to the flight deck, to be hosed down with fresh water and re-hangared.

Edinburgh returned to Scapa Flow, and we relaxed by playing deck hockey. HMS *Hood*, the largest battlecruiser in the Navy, was moored fairly close. She had a wonderfully large quarterdeck ideal for deck hockey and we started an intership tournament. After a few days we sailed into the Atlantic and on 22 May 1941 off the Bay of Biscay intercepted the German steamship *Lech*, which scuttled herself. Meanwhile *Hood* sailed to hunt the German battleship *Bismarck*, which had disappeared into the Denmark Strait. On 24 May *Hood* sighted *Bismarck*, closed until she was in range, and both ships opened fire more or less at the same time. At about the third salvo from the

Bismarck at extreme range, one of her shells hit the *Hood* almost vertically and penetrated her decks straight into the magazine. All that was seen was a huge pall of smoke in the distance and the *Hood* sank, on 27 May, with only three survivors. *Edinburgh* was ordered north to join the Home Fleet in the hunt for *Bismarck* and took a minor part in the battle which led on 27 May to the German being destroyed.[14]

Years later I discovered a picture of the *Hood* in Boldre church just outside Lymington, this being the family church her captain attended.

3

BEACHMASTER, RN

In August 1941 I was transferred off the *Edinburgh* to Cape Town on a merchant ship to join the battlecruiser HMS *Repulse*,[15] and then off Mombasa on 8 September 1941 I was transferred to the battleship HMS *Revenge*, where I became sub lieutenant of the gunroom.[16] After a spell in Mombasa we sailed for Trincomalee in Ceylon where I managed to see my father, who was Naval Transport Officer. After Ceylon we headed for Mauritius where I bought fresh limes for the gunroom. Because of an excessive use of fresh water due to boiler leaks we headed to Durban for repairs, where a generous person, Mr Alexander, offered to take six officers for a break on his farm. He met me at Merryvale railway station and took me home to meet his wife and his daughter Joan, who subsequently became a good friend. He was a charming man who had lost a leg in the First World War. They had a number of horses on the farm and one that had just been broken in.

Whether it was wise to put me, a naval officer, on a newly broken-in horse I do not know. However, the animal started galloping up a pathway between the neighbouring farm and the Alexanders', and when a large branch loomed in the way, I put my arm up and stupidly caught it in the branch. I was jerked off the horse and my right elbow was broken. With a greenstick fracture on my left wrist I was driven by old Alexander to the nearest military hospital where the doctors said I would have to have my arm amputated. Alexander would have none of this and drove me to Maritzburg where I was taken to the

Oribi Hospital. Luckily there was a Nuffield specialist on duty who immediately took me in hand. I was given a full anaesthetic and eventually woke up humming 'The Sheikh of Araby'. The arm had been set and the greenstick fracture had a splint, so back I went to the farm.

After a few days I returned to Durban and on 23 September 1942 was put ashore on medical grounds, having been paid off from the *Revenge* and billeted in Fleet House. I had to go from there to the Addington Hospital where the nurses used to hang a small weight on my right hand to try and straighten it. Gradually I managed to almost completely straighten my arm but it has never been quite as good as it was originally. Whilst based in Durban I worked at HMS *Afrikander IV* in the RATES office (the Admiralty training establishment) in West Street where there was an Admiral Scott, a pleasant man.[17] My job was to inspect plans for a new base to be built on the Bluff. It was a ridiculous job because I had not the faintest idea of what I should or should not approve.

One day the admiral sent for me and said, 'The drafting commander has gone on three weeks' leave and during his absence you are to be the drafting officer.' I went back to Fleet House that evening in high spirits and said to Dick Bainbridge, who had become a good friend, 'We are going home.' He asked me how I knew and I explained that I was the new drafting officer and the first two people to be drafted would be us. Dick was convalescing from lung damage sustained at Tobruk. Sure enough, within ten days the troopship *Britannic* was due to dock in Durban on her way to the United Kingdom with a considerable number of Italian prisoners aboard and I had nominated Dick and me to be repatriated on the ship.[18]

On the ship's arrival I took Dick to the admiral's office, and we both knocked and went in. Scott, who was rather clueless himself, said, 'What can I do for you, boys?' I said, 'Well, sir, we have come to say goodbye.' He said, 'What has happened to you?' I said, 'We have been drafted.' 'Oh,' he said, 'I am sorry to lose you, have a good trip', and off we went.

We sailed well out into the Atlantic and eventually turned eastwards, docking at Liverpool. Before leaving Durban I had bought a long bag of sugar to take home with me as I knew there would be little in England. While walking down the quay in Liverpool with my bag of sugar over my shoulder, I was stopped by a policeman who said, 'Excuse me, sir, but I think you are losing your sugar.' The bag had a slit in it and the sugar was starting to trickle on to the quay. I saved the rest and took it to London with me. On arrival I reported to the Admiralty at Queen Anne's Mansions and was asked where the hell had I come from.

I explained I had been drafted from Durban, and the officer-in-charge said, 'Who the hell drafted you?' 'I don't know,' I explained. Looking through my file, he said, 'I see you volunteered for special service. Did you mean it?'

It was true that whilst in Durban, with a pretty girl next to me in the cinema, seeing the newsreels of the Malta convoys and full of bravado, I had volunteered for special service. Now, being confronted with reality and the Admiralty officer asking 'Did you mean it?', there was nothing else I could say but 'Yes, sir.'

On 18 March 1943, after a short leave I became a trainee beachmaster in charge of G Commando at HMS *Armadillo*, a cold grey stone building at Ardentinny on the shores of Loch Long in Scotland. In each commando, in addition to the beachmaster, there were two sub lieutenants. Our job was to go ashore in the first wave aboard an LCA (Landing Craft, Assault) and with my men secure the beach for the next wave of infantry. This involved assault courses, a 52-mile route march and unarmed combat. On completion of training we embarked on the troopship *Circassia* in the Gare Loch together with a large number of the army. In early July we set sail in company with the troopship *Durban Castle* and another ship, first out into the Atlantic and then south and into the Mediterranean.

At this stage none of us had any idea where we were going until one evening two sub lieutenants and I were given our orders that we would be landing the next morning, 10 July 1943, on the south-east coast of Sicily at Pachino in preparation for the Allied invasion. Our orders advised us that a large water tower at Pachino would be illuminated by the RAF and would serve as our landmark. That night a fairly strong wind blew up with a rough sea. Our orders stipulated that we would board the landing craft held in davits and use the water tower, hopefully illuminated, as our point of arrival. We all blackened our faces and I must say that we were a little frightened. When the LCAs were slipped and the coxswain steered on the given course for Pachino, there was no sign of the water tower. The RAF had not only illuminated it but knocked it down. As we arrived near the beach there were cries coming from the water and two American doctors were picked up who had dropped by parachute, along with another group of Americans from North Africa. With typical American efficiency they had jumped by parachute at least a quarter of a mile offshore.

My position was just behind the ramp and I was to be the first man ashore, together with two leading seamen who each had port and starboard lights that were placed on the beach to guide the next wave of landing craft. When we landed ashore an Italian raised his arms in surrender by a small beach hut, but sadly we shot him and there were no other apparent residents. The lights were set up and the next wave of landing craft came in with the army and up and out of the beach. I took over the small hut as my headquarters and we buried the poor Italian about 50 feet away. The army eventually brought in troops in DUKWs[19] and by daylight there was a steady stream of army units passing up the beach. My commando unit held its position on the beach with an occasional night attack by German aircraft. By this time we all had our slit trenches and there were no casualties. What I will never forget is after about two days three Italian women came down to the beach to my hut and enquired of the Italian who had been there. We showed them where he was buried and they proceeded to dig him up with wails and crying. I felt terrible. They asked if they could take him away for burial, which we gladly allowed them to do.

To the west of Pachino, the Americans had landed at Gela and round the eastern tip of Sicily the British had landed at Syracuse. We eventually all moved up through Sicily. I took my commando to Lentini to await further orders. Commander Scott who ran our headquarters told me that we were being moved across by an LST (Landing Ship, Tank) to Bone in North Africa for a spell. This was a tented camp in an olive grove with very little to do. I decided one day to go up the coast in my amphibious jeep to Tunis. Here there was a NAAFI and I bought a very smart pair of brown boots that became my pride and joy.

Back in the camp at Bone we found a vehicle dump nearby and several of the chaps picked up private vehicles, which we all worked on. When we eventually moved back to cross over to Sicily we were a very motley band with our own transport. Arriving back in Sicily, we were taken to Taormina which is just before Messina and at the time there were beautiful flowering creepers hanging from a large wall. Going north about half a mile to Messina we were overcome by a horrible smell of rotting bodies. It appeared there had been an attack by Allied forces, when they arrived there, against the escaping Germans who were evacuating their last foothold in Sicily. We were told they had taken up positions in the high land above Reggio, on the other side of the Strait of Messina. We assembled at Taormina and were told we would be proceeding across the Strait of Messina to Reggio into the toe of Italy and would be boarding the LCAs the following night at Taormina. I had all my gear in my amphibious jeep with my driver Able Seaman Waugh. I told him to drive the jeep aboard one of the LSTs the following day and report to me on the beach. Early in the morning of 3 September 1943 I boarded our LCA with my G Commando and headed across the Strait of Messina. It was a lovely clear night with a calm sea and we encountered no problems whatsoever. As we landed on the beach at Reggio there was no opposition but as it started to get light the Germans opened up from the hill above the town, but thank God they could not depress their 88 mm guns low enough to hit the beach. However, they could in fact strafe the LSTs when they landed later that morning. We cleared a path up the beach, having swept it for mines, and put down the white cloth strips as a safe path out for the army.

About half an hour after the landing a voice said, 'Have a cup of coffee, sir.' It was AB Waugh, with my jeep, who had brewed some coffee on the small stove we carried. On being asked how the hell he had arrived so early, he replied, 'Well, sir, it was such a nice calm night I thought we would drive over from Taormina to Reggio', which he had done.

As I mentioned, the beachmaster was in complete command of the beach during a landing and it was our duty as G Commando to ensure a safe path off the beach into the hinterland. At about half past ten that morning when the large vehicles were landing from the LSTs a DUKW motored up the beach and stopped at the exit road from the beach. On board was General Montgomery with some of his staff. We had learnt that he was a great one for haranguing the troops. He stopped and of course was surrounded by some of our army and started haranguing them. This was contrary to regulations, as my job as beachmaster was to ensure a continuous flow of vehicles off the beach.

I went up to him and during a pause in his oration said, 'Excuse me, sir, would you mind vacating the beach?'

He said, 'Who the hell are you?'

I said, 'Sir, I am the beachmaster in full command of everything that goes on on this beach and I am sorry, sir, but it is essential you leave the beach.'

He said a few more words to the troops and then I was pleased to see he moved on. That was my only direct contact with Montgomery during the war and I had the impression that he was an arrogant man. However, overall he turned out to be a very successful general.

When a few weeks later we arrived at Termoli on the east coast of Italy we found this was as far as we were destined to go in the near future, as the Germans had taken up a line about five miles north of the town.[20] Italy collapsed and the Italians surrendered in September 1943 to the Allies, and the various prisoner-of-war camps previously guarded by them had their gates opened and many of the British prisoners walked out into the countryside. After a short time, however, the Germans moved in and re-established control. Most of the prisoners who had escaped took to the hills and the Italian peasants around the countryside helped to shelter a large number. Commander Nichol in charge of G Commando told us to bring in as many escapees as possible.

Two MAS boats (Motoscafo Armato Silurante, an Italian motor torpedo boat or MTB) arrived and moored at the end of the quay. These were built of wood and had three Isotta Fraschini engines. The centre engine had the ability to alter its exhaust from being straight through and very noisy into an underwater exhaust that was relatively silent and capable of doing 12 knots on its own. Italian crews manned these MASs but each carried two British army officers to ensure the Italians stayed loyal to us. A recce up the coast was done in one of them and we crept on to a deserted beach. Two of my men came ashore with me in the dinghy and we wandered into the countryside, not knowing what to expect. We came across a small Italian farmhouse and roused the occupants.

A very frightened woman appeared, whispered 'Tedeschi' to us, and pointed to behind the house. Obviously some Germans had bedded down there for the night. We said 'Grazie' to the woman, and crept back to the MAS.

We noticed that the riverbeds up the coast were dry and formed an obvious area British escaped prisoners of war could use to come down before boarding their rescue craft. By now it was October 1943. We carried out several more night recces up the coast and noticed that a train pulled out of one of the stations regularly at half past three in the morning. It was decided that Termoli was to be our base and the next little town behind the lines up the coast was Ortona. This was followed by Pescara further up, and then Ancona which had a small port and was easy to recognise because there was a hill behind the town.

There was a small restaurant down near the quay in Termoli in which we used to meet and discuss our plans over a glass of rather indifferent Italian wine. There was no light in the evenings as the Germans could have strafed us, and so our discussions were held by candlelight – all very cloak and dagger. Two army officers used to join us: one was the cartoonist 'Giles' of the *Daily Telegraph*, who always had pictures of pretty girls in his cartoons, and the other was an army officer about my age named Roy Farran.[21] We all decided that the only way to rescue our prisoners was at a chosen area at the end of the dried riverbed. A small group would be landed at a specified point and would go up into the hills and gather as many prisoners as possible. At a predetermined time several days later the prisoners would be herded down to the pick-up spot. The rescue party would arrive by one of the

MAS boats and, having flashed a torch signal ashore, would wait for an answering signal to verify who was answering. We would then put a dinghy ashore and pick them up. During my time there I found these small rescue operations quite emotional, as frequently those being rescued would kiss the deck and put their arms around us in thanks.

We discovered after a couple of weeks that the Germans would come down with a small radar van in an endeavour to close down these missions and we were obliged to establish pick-up areas further and further along the coast. One day Roy Farran approached me and said he had instructions to blow up a bridge on the coast road some 60 miles north of Termoli and asked if we would take him and his party. I told him I would. On the appointed day we boarded one of the MASs and proceeded up the coast at full speed until ready to turn west, when we would stop the two outboard engines and creep in with our single underwater-exhaust centre engine.

On this particular night as we crept in towards the beach, we stopped as usual and used our binoculars to check that everything was all clear. As I was looking through my binoculars the hair on my neck stood up and I realised that there was some sort of craft near the shore. Both Roy Farran and I came to the conclusion that it was a submarine on the surface charging its batteries, and the submarine was obviously not one of ours. The area Roy Farran wanted was a little to the south of this position and so we left and crept south before landing his party. After arriving back at Termoli I broke radio silence and reported to C.-in-C. Taranto what we had seen. We understood a couple of days later that Roy Farran had blown up his bridge and that an Allied aircraft had sunk the submarine which was still there and obviously had had engine trouble. This incident is mentioned in Roy Farran's book *Winged Dagger*.[22]

The C.-in-C. Taranto asked us whether it would be possible to capture a German prisoner for interrogation. We found the Germans were in the habit of sending a despatch-rider down the coast to their forward position just north of Termoli and I knew of an ideal area to obtain what was needed. Some areas on the road were very poor and the Germans were apt to put up a sign 'SS' which I think meant 'diversion'. One of these signs was copied and we took the MAS to a point where we knew there was a sharp bend in the road. The sign was put up together with white tapes leading off towards a pebbly area near the beach, and the MAS lay off, with two men standing near the diversion sign. Nothing happened the first night and we came back empty-handed. On the following night we hit the jackpot! Two of G Commando stood by the diversion sign and, lo and behold, a German motorcyclist duly arrived, skidded to a halt and tried to go onto the pebbly track. Our two chaps set on him, pulled his tin helmet over his eyes and donked him on the back of the head. He was then ushered down to the dinghy, taken aboard and locked up. We removed the sign and the tapes and then wheeled his motorbike down to the beach, into the dinghy and eventually aboard the MAS. After a brief inspection of the beach to ensure that everything was shipshape we returned to Termoli. I don't know what happened to the wretched German but he was taken away to an army area for interrogation. I still have a slight scar on my thumb from trying to ride the motorbike when I caught it in the handlebars!

On another evening we were due to pick up a party of escaped prisoners from a beach in a bay up the coast. As it turned out we were very lucky in that the two MAS boats were temporarily out of service and an LCI (Landing Craft, Infantry) was put at our disposal. This had a high freeboard and half the speed of our MASs. When we arrived off the rendezvous point the agreed signal was flashed ashore, but there was no reply. We decided, however, to put a dinghy ashore and I climbed into it with two other crew and started pulling ashore. Halfway to the shore we were fired at from a point in the northern part of the bay and it was most unnerving to see tracer bullets coming towards us and at the last moment going over our heads. My immediate reaction was to go backwards over the side of the boat into the water – as it turned out, a wise decision. Luckily the captain of the LCI went astern to cover us from the enemy bullets. I and one other got alongside the LCI and were quickly hauled aboard. This taught me a sharp lesson: don't go in if your signal is not answered. The operation for the night was abandoned and we returned to Termoli and on the way had a good tot of Pusser's Rum. This confirmed our view that the Germans were keeping a good lookout round the coast.

A touching little thing happened one day when, rashly, I decided to go in the amphibious jeep towards the front line. An army officer immediately stopped me and said, 'Get to hell out of here.' The next moment a mortar shell came down and I realised this was no place for me. Going back, there was an area where the wounded were being held, including a German whose eyes were bandaged, and he was obviously in very poor shape. A kind British Tommy came up, lit a cigarette, put it in his hand and said: 'Here you are, mate.'

On a final occasion before the trip up to Chioggia,[23] I did a recce past Ancona. I crept in towards Ancona to get my bearings and saw that there were many dark shapes forming off the coast. I realised it was some sort of convoy forming up to go across towards Yugoslavia. I turned off, charged up the air bottles to fire the torpedoes and then let go both at the largest black object and scored two direct hits. By this time I was going full speed back to Termoli and, after we got in, our chaps patted me on the back. The next morning I was ordered to go to C.-in-C.'s office in Taranto. Everybody said, 'Goodo, you will get a gong.' I arrived at C.-in-C.'s office, was kept waiting, and then a captain came out and said, 'Right, go in.' I received the biggest dressing down of all time. Evidently intelligence knew all about the convoy and there was a destroyer waiting for it some distance off pointing at the target. This had blown the gaff. My reward was a loss of six-month seniority and a strong warning from C.-in-C. Taranto that we should keep well clear of everything that might involve other units.

Needless to say, I was mentioned in despatches for my efforts in rescuing escaped prisoners. This appeared in the *London Gazette* on 27 April 1944. Our little sorties up the coast started to attract various people who wanted to watch the proceedings. One of these was a charming Italian priest who had been a padre in a prison camp just south of Venice. He told us that when the camps had been opened many of the prisoners had escaped to the Venice area and he believed that if we landed him in the vicinity he could make contact and get them out safely. After one of our candlelight and wine discussions in

Termoli we considered the only way to effect this was to have a base roughly abeam Venice but over on one of the islands. Lussin Piccolo was chosen. I advised Taranto that if possible we would appreciate a little air cover due to the distance from Termoli to Venice, which meant our return would be mainly in daylight. After this was approved, a few days later I took the priest up in our MAS, got a fix off the hill behind Ancona, then crossed the mouth of the River Po. I duly dropped off the priest in his black habit, just south of Venice. As it grew light on our return trip it was heartening to occasionally see one of our aircraft appearing. We altered course off the Tremiti Islands to Termoli.

4

THE BATTLE OF LUSSIN PICCOLO

O ur next destination was Lussin Piccolo, which is 'Little Lussin' in English, in Croatia.[24] We had with us a Croatian who had been imprisoned by the Italians on the Tremiti Islands and only got away when Italy was on the verge of collapse. The decision to go to Lussin Piccolo in early November 1943 was made not by me but by our superiors in the C.-in-C.'s office. The obvious route was to go way out into the Adriatic from Termoli towards the Tremiti Islands and head north. Both our fishing boats were filled with rations for the people we hoped to rescue and the decks were packed up to the guard rails with jerrycans of high octane petrol for the MASs which were to be sent up to us. As we slowly laboured up the Adriatic, I sat by the mast on jerrycans of petrol and slowly realised that if German aircraft attacked us we were a floating bomb. During the first night we were separated from Guy Morgan, a special war correspondent, and it was only when we stopped for a time the following afternoon that he hove in sight.[25] Lussin Piccolo came into view just after sunset and we arrived alongside the quay of the main town just after dark.

We were boarded by Tito's partisans, armed to the teeth with every type of weapon, and one who spoke English said to me, 'Last year the Czechniks were here', they being the royalists, and he proudly announced, 'We attacked them, slit the throats of 173 and threw their bodies into the sea.'

John Worsley, a war artist, whispered to me, 'I think we may have come to the wrong place.'[26]

Worsley, Guy Morgan and I were taken with a partisan escort to a villa in a small bay in the south-west part of the island. We were told to make ourselves comfortable in the delightful villa owned, as we eventually found out, by the Cosulich family,[27] who owned the Lloyd Triestino shipping line.[28] Here, stranded by the war, were the chairman's attractive wife Carmen and her pretty daughter Noretta, who played the guitar and sang in a quiet way.

The partisans unloaded the rations from the two fishing vessels and stowed them in an empty hotel just behind our house. We rescued a couple of cartons and Carmen Cosulich insisted on cooking for us. Noretta, the daughter, laid the table for us and we insisted that they join us for dinner. Sadly, this ideal set-up did not last for long. Three of the partisans came down to the villa and virtually interrogated us, but it was obvious they wanted the food. After two days the partisans threw out the Cosulich mother and daughter and I will never forget them leaving with their sole possession, a live chicken in a string basket. The three partisans obviously wanted to move into the house but I was adamant, supported by John and Guy, that we did not want them. The only uniform we had included rather heavy commando boots and we decided to cover the parquet floors with army blankets to protect the house. In the meantime I buried in a flowerbed in the garden 100 gold sovereigns I had been issued with, it being an acceptable currency worldwide. Years later I returned with my son Nicholas in the hope of finding them, but alas no luck.

Another visitor was a very well-spoken man with an American accent who I believe, all these years later, might well have been a German. He told us he had to go to Tito's headquarters and would return for us. After about six days at this lovely villa I woke up about five o'clock in the morning of 13 November to hear the sound of craft in the distance. I dressed and hurried down the path to the little bay to see about eight small dots approaching and behind them the shape of a large vessel. I realised these were landing craft, rushed back to the house and woke John and Guy. We all got dressed and I led them, with our tommy guns and a little extra ammunition, round the inside end of the bay. Opposite our villa there was a low wall. We crouched behind the wall and it became clear the landing craft were coming straight into the bay towards us. I said to John, 'Don't open fire until I say so.' In these situations one cannot help feeling quite afraid.

One of the landing craft came straight for the shore in front of us and when it was a couple of hundred feet away I said 'Fire!' As we did so bodies were falling out into the water and the landing craft sheered away. We later discovered that our invaders were a unit of the elite SS Gebirgsjäger, an alpine division of the SS, and we had killed sixteen of them. We retired and crept into the woods and took up another position. After a while we heard the sound of vehicles being unloaded and decided it was no time to be British any more. We went through the woods to a small port on the other side with a fishing vessel alongside, and joined a number of partisans trying to start the vessel. The engine proved to be a hot bulb diesel, which you have to heat with a blowlamp before starting. Eventually we got under way, with the decks loaded with partisans heading towards the Yugoslav coast. A little later two German Arado Ar 196 seaplanes appeared and strafed us in turn. Each plane dived down towards us, firing its wing guns. Behind the pilot there was a rotating turret for the observer, who opened up as the aircraft turned away in a wide circle prior to coming down again. John, Guy and I got down to the engine room and crouched behind the engine to avoid the bullets. We crept round the engine to a safe position as the aircraft passed. The partisans on deck were being decimated by the gunfire and most of those remaining jumped into the sea in an attempt to swim to a small island in the bay. They had left a machine gun on deck but I found it had jammed and was of no use. The bullets fired from the two seaplanes were incendiaries, and on one of the attacks poor Guy was hit in the arm. John and I saw his arm bend almost double where the bone had been shot away.

On looking up through the engine room porthole we saw a large naval vessel approaching and realised we had no chance of getting to Yugoslavia before being shot to bits. On one attack an Arado dropped a small bomb that exploded by the bow of the old fishing vessel, and it started to sink. We decided to surrender and John found a piece of white cloth that we tied to the wheelhouse and put the engine out of gear. An old Yugoslavian naval cruiser eventually pulled up alongside us and we were taken aboard by the Germans. As we pulled away we realised the fishing boat was sinking fairly fast. I turned to one of the German officers and said, 'Ich bin ein englischer Offizier von der Kriegsmarine.' The Germans immediately took us down and a doctor put Guy Morgan to bed with a splint on his arm, and we were given a very edible meal of wurst and sauerkraut.

5

PRISONER OF WAR

B y this time the wind had got up and as the cruiser continued to patrol in the bay we started to roll heavily. Most of the German crew, who were obviously not used to this, became quite seasick but luckily we felt quite all right. Twenty-four hours later we were landed at Pola, taken over by the German army and treated in a very rough way. We were shut in a large warehouse with a stone floor, without food or water, and lay on the stone floor throughout the night.

Guy Morgan's arm began to look in a bad way and he was taken off

Marlag camp

for treatment by the Germans. It was the last time we saw him till his arrival in the naval prison camp at Marlag, where we were all eventually locked up. The next day, still without food, John and I were put in the back of an army lorry with canvas sides and an open tail. We were guarded by young German troops and slowly drove up the mountain road away from Pola. In our training we were always taught that the best chance of escape was in the first twenty-four hours after capture and I told John that I must try and get back to Termoli. I asked one of the young German guards if I could sit on the tailgate and wash my face in the rain. They asked me how I came to speak a little German. I had taken German at School Certificate level at Ampleforth. I said my mother was half-German. They became very friendly and asked me if I was all right. The rough track out of Moskana had numerous curves and the driver was forced to slow to a crawl to get round the corners. As we got to a corner just outside the village I grabbed the roof structure, pulled myself up and dropped down on to the road behind the lorry. John took it as a cue to start shouting to attract the guards' attention and as I got up to dive over the side of the road into the bushes one of the guards fired his rifle and the bullet nicked me in the palm of my hand. I ran as fast as I could down the mountainside amongst the undergrowth of bushes and the Germans let go a fusillade of shots in my direction. About 150 yards down I crawled into the undergrowth and buried myself under a pile of dead leaves. I could hear the guards hunting around looking for me and I felt sure that they could hear my heart beating. However, they stopped searching for me and I heard the lorry disappearing. I did not dare to move until dark and then crawled further down the hillside, crossed a small river, which was extremely cold, and crept up the other side of the hill into the village.

We were always told that if we escaped, go to the church priest who would look after you. I found the church, knocked on the door and eventually it was opened by a priest. I said, 'Prisonnier anglais'. He did not want to know and shut the door in my face. I must have looked a very odd sight with my hand pouring with blood and my face covered in scratches from the brambles on the hillside. I decided the safest thing to do was to walk back the way I had come, and after walking about two miles in the pouring rain I turned up a hillside road and found a small hamlet. I picked up a handful of pebbles and threw them at the window of one of the houses. After a moment the window was opened and I said, in a sort of loud whisper, 'Prisonnier anglais'. A couple came down in their nightclothes and lit a nasty-smelling carbide lamp. They were wonderful to me, took me in, cleaned me down, bound up my hand and put a mattress at the foot of their double bed, where I went out like a light. The next morning they brought me some breakfast and a youngish man came in to see if he could be of any assistance. The owners of the cottage were Slavs and had no time for the Italians. I was in my commando uniform and the beautiful pair of boots. The young man wisely said I must change and eventually appeared with a selection of old clothes and rough boots with a hole in the sole of one of them, and my red hair was shaved off. I had hidden in my uniform some Italian money and asked if they could sell me a bicycle. The young man disappeared and eventually came back with a rough old bicycle and took off both tyres and patched up the inner tubes, which he did by lunchtime. They asked me where I was going and I said, 'Per Trieste.' Later that afternoon he took me over the mountain with my old bicycle and indicated a road on the other side that would eventually take me up to Trieste.

A sequel to this incident happened in the mid-1960s when the Yugoslav Shipping Line, who were members of the East African Conference Line, invited my wife Margaret and me to visit them in Trieste. While motoring there from Rejika we located the small hamlet and asked two women who were pounding rice where I could find two people who had helped a British prisoner of war in 1943. They pointed to a small cottage, which I recognised, where I knocked on the door. An elderly couple welcomed us with great happiness and hospitality. As we were leaving, a tractor appeared and stopped, the driver leapt off and engulfed us in an enormous embrace – it was the young man who had provided me with the bicycle and helped me over the mountains to Trieste. It was a truly wonderful reunion.

I got down to the road, mounted my bicycle and within a hundred yards both wheels punctured and I threw the bicycle into the ditch. Saturated by the rain, I walked up the road and came to another cottage and again knocked on the door. An old man appeared and took me in. The house was very basic with a single large room, an open fire and a ladder up to a platform where he obviously slept. He offered me some raw potato to eat and then beckoned to follow him. We went to the back of the house where there was a hayloft and he indicated I should sleep there. The hay was warm and eventually I stopped shivering and dried out. The next morning I crept out fairly early and started up the road that I hoped would lead to Trieste. By lunchtime I had pulled up a swede from a field, rubbed it to get all the dirt off, and ate it. I continued my journey and about two o'clock came to a small village, where I sat down near a house, wondering what the next move would be.

An old woman saw me, disappeared then reappeared with a cup of warm milk, which was delicious. She asked me where I was going and I said, 'Per Trieste.' She said, 'Momento', walked up the road and returned with an Italian to whom I took an instant dislike. He had a rucksack on his back and asked me if I had any money. I showed him some Italian lire. He took several notes and disappeared down the road, where I later realised there was a railway station. He came back, gave me my ticket and indicated we should go. Shortly after arriving at the station a small train with wooden bench seats arrived and we boarded. To my horror there were several German soldiers sitting in the carriage and off we trundled towards Trieste. As it was getting dark the train stopped at a station on the outskirts of Trieste. The Italian indicated that I should get out and follow him. We walked up a couple of streets, came to a house and the Italian rang the doorbell. One of the family opened the door and we went into a kitchen where a meal was in progress. I sat down and was given a delicious plate of stew and dumplings. They quizzed me about what I was doing and I tried to explain in broken Italian that I was an escaped British naval officer trying to get to Termoli.

None of them spoke a word of English and after a while my rucksack acquaintance took me out to the back and into a hayloft where he indicated I should sleep. As he left me I heard the door being locked and I started to worry in case I wanted to get out. About one o'clock in the morning he reappeared and said, 'Subito, subito, tedeschi', the Italian for Germans. I was so befuddled, having been in a deep sleep, that I wondered how the Germans could be in the outskirts of Trieste at one o'clock in the morning. He led me to the end of the street that turned at right angles and as I went into it two men shouted, 'Hände hoch!' For a moment I felt sorry for the Italian but, on looking round, realised he was no longer there and it was only then the penny dropped that I had been sold. The two Germans were in plain clothes with herringbone overcoats and the leading one, who levelled a revolver, wore pebble-lens glasses.

Again, in one's training, one was told that if one wanted to distract a person one must look away slightly to one side and show surprise, and the other person would certainly look round as well. I did this with great success, and as the wearer of the pebble-lenses looked round I kicked him with all my strength in the balls. He collapsed on the ground in agony. I reached down for the revolver, followed by the other German. Being only twenty-two years old and fit, I grabbed the revolver and shot both of them. With the reverberation of the noise from the revolver, I just ran. After about five minutes I reached a roadblock and was stopped. The soldier there said, 'Dove andate?' (Where are you going?) I was bundled into a Citroën car with a German sitting next to me and driven to a building which I later realised was the Gestapo office. A German woman in a grey uniform with a swastika and eagle on her bosom sat with a notebook and standing either side of me were two German *Feldwebel* or NCOs. I was asked my name, to which I replied, 'Giuseppe Lorino' and pretended to be French. The interrogation continued in detail: where was I born, in which street, what was my father doing, and the interrogation was interrupted with one of the Germans at my side digging his elbow into my ribs and shouting, 'What is your name?' I pretended not to understand, saying again I was French, and after a delay another German was produced who spoke schoolboy French. Having been born and lived in Belgium, my French was far better than his. After a prolonged interrogation I was marched out and into a cell with a straw mattress and a stone toilet in the corner. The door slammed and I lay down shivering and cold on the mattress. I then realised that were I to be identified as the person who had shot the two Gestapo I was in for a very unpleasant death.

Next morning I was again taken out and the interrogation repeated: 'What is your name? Where were you born?' etc. Inevitably, as the interrogation proceeded some of the details I gave were not the same as those previously given and I was bundled back into my cell followed by five German women in their grey uniforms. I was stripped naked and the women proceeded to beat me with flexible rubber truncheons and obviously relished what they were doing. I tried not to make a noise and fell to the ground after a minute or two whereupon one of the *Feldwebel* stamped on my right hand and smashed my right thumbnail. After some more beating I was left alone, the cell door slammed and I crawled on to my mattress. I was frightened that if I said I was an English officer they might have put two and two together, linking me to the Italian who had sold me. The interrogation was repeated the next day with interruptions of 'What is your name?' in English. I was taken back to my cell and given a further beating and then left alone, by which time I was so sore I could barely crawl on to the mattress. There I lay until morning when I was again hauled out. By this time I was in such a state that I said, 'I am a British officer', and for causing trouble I was given a further beating. I could no longer stand and lay in considerable pain on my cell mattress.

Later that afternoon a German officer arrived, lifted me up and carried me to his car. He spoke perfect English, said he was driving me to their headquarters and apologised for my condition. He told me his name was Helmut Pirner from the SS Gebirgsjäger, the unit that had landed at Lussin Piccolo. He told me he had lived in Wimbledon for seventeen years before the war and took me to their headquarters at Abbatsia, near Fiume, which today is Rejika. He carried me into what had been a smart hotel and to a bedroom on the first floor. The room was spotless and he carefully placed me on the bed, which had white linen sheets. Within five minutes the door opened and the colonel of the regiment accompanied by another officer stood near the bed, and they clicked their heels to attention with a slight Germanic bow. The colonel said, 'Herr Leutnant, we apologise for what has happened to you; this would not have occurred in this regiment. As you cannot walk and therefore cannot escape, if you are prepared to give us your parole for twenty-four hours, you are a guest of our mess.' At that time all I wanted to do was turn to the wall and die. They brought schnapps, some wurst and sauerkraut and had a party in my room. Eventually I was left alone and, having drunk a considerable amount of schnapps, turned to the wall and fell asleep.

The next morning Helmut Pirner arrived, sat down by my bed and told me he and his family lived in Mauerkirchen Strasse in Munich, and he seriously hoped the war would not last too much longer. I was well looked after that day and gradually tried to start walking. The greatest pain was from my balls which were swollen and black from the beating by the German women. The following day Helmut Pirner again arrived and said he had been told to drive me to Ljubljana in Yugoslavia where he understood John Worsley was imprisoned. As we went through the roads in the forest I secretly hoped the partisans might attack us, but eventually we arrived at the prison in Ljubljana and was given a hearty goodbye handshake by Helmut Pirner. Sure enough, John Worsley was looking out of a window. There in a large courtyard prisoners were being made to jog round with packs of sand on their backs. If one fell he was clubbed with a rifle butt and forced to get up again. John told me he thought some of them were Russians.

A couple of days later four old decrepit German guards appeared to take us to Germany by train. The only conversation consisted of them saying, 'Krieg ist nicht gut, alles ist Scheiss, ich habe eine Frau und Kinder.' (War is no good, everything's shitty, I've got a wife and kids.) We trundled slowly across Germany, eventually arriving in Berlin at the Lehrter Bahnhof on the evening of 22 November, by which time John and I were very hungry and our guards queued up with us for a 'Stammessen', which was the only meal available in Germany without ration cards. This comprised the inevitable wurst and sauerkraut.

Before we reached the head of the queue, however, the air raid sirens went, and in the ensuing turmoil of Teutonic shouting we were bundled down some stone steps and into a concrete shelter with many other Germans. This, we found out subsequently, was a 1,000-bomber raid by the Allies, and strange to say we believed that as they were our bombs they would not hurt us. I was near the door of the shelter, as the German civilians had pushed themselves into the far corner of the shelter. Suddenly, to our horror, down the steps clattered an incendiary bomb, hissing at one end. My survival instinct took over. I jumped up, again mysteriously believing that as it was one of ours it would not hurt us. I picked up the non-hissing end and threw it back up the stairs.

Little did I know at the time that the Bahnhof or railway station, which was so badly damaged, was less than a hundred yards from the entrance to Hitler's bunker. He eventually committed suicide there with Eva Braun and their bodies were later burnt outside. Next morning after the raid our four guards gathered the two of us together, took us back to the remains of the station and marched us out into the street. There was considerable destruction all around with vehicles blown up, including one in a tree. Our guards said, 'Bahnhof kaput', and headed north. As we were being marched along by old German soldiers the local women realised we were prisoners and came out and spat in our faces. This hatred was most unnerving and the poor old guards tried to protect us.

After a long march to the outskirts of Berlin, we arrived at another uncomfortable prison at Oranienburg, administered by an unpleasant group of guards.[29] Most of the prisoners were Russian and being treated like animals. I remember looking at an area nearby and saw a British officer in uniform. I gave him a wave and he was so scared that he ducked out of sight. Thank God, that evening our four old guards appeared with the usual, 'Komm, komm, aufstehen!' (Come on, come on, get out!) and marched us from this dreadful place to a local railway station where we boarded another train. Our old guards, who stayed in the carriage with us, fell asleep, leaving John and me sitting between them. One of these old Germans had been quite unpleasant, whereas the other three had been very reasonable to us. John noticed that the unpleasant one sitting next to him had his bayonet in its holster on its side, and he managed to extract it quietly and throw it out of the window. History does not relate what happened to the guard.

We eventually arrived at a small station named Westertimke in Lower Saxony and marched through the woods to what turned out to be a Dulag, short for *Durchgangslager* or interrogation centre.[30] The Dulag was very basic, with each person in their little cell with the inevitable woven wood mattress and one blanket. Our daily ration was a cup of German ersatz coffee for breakfast, a minute plate of sauerkraut with a little piece of wurst, and for our evening meal another mug of coffee. If you wanted to go to the toilet you banged on the door and called out 'Posten, Abort.' We were generally kept waiting and eventually escorted out to very basic latrines where the guard waited. We found out that the Geneva Convention stipulated that prison cells should have adequate heating. Each of our cells had a minute fireplace that each received a single briquette of coal, and any heat disappeared after a couple of hours. By evening our cells became extremely cold. After a month of incarceration without access to other prisoners we were finally taken out for interrogation, in my case by a German naval lieutenant named Liebel who spoke good English with a slight American accent.

My first interrogation started with Liebel asking if I would like a cigarette and I said, 'I do not smoke.' He then said, 'Would you like a little drink?' The answer of course was 'Yes' and a glass of schnapps appeared out of nowhere. I realised this was a softener to make me talk. Under the Geneva Convention a prisoner had to give his name, rank and number and nothing else. I gave my name and rank and said, 'As an officer I do not have a number.'

Liebel said, 'I have to tell you that yours is a very serious case and there has been a request for your transfer to Berlin. We do know that many that go to Berlin do not come back.'

I was then questioned about my remit, the various landing craft employed, their capacity, speed etc., to which I gave greatly exaggerated performances. I think Liebel must have realised this but after a few days' interrogation he became very pleasant, said he had served in America and had been in the German navy. Eventually after eight weeks John Worsley reappeared and we were marched out of the woods to the gates of Marlag 'O', being short for Marine Lager, the naval prison camp.[31] I had been so haunted by the fear that the Germans would link me to the two Gestapo I had shot that I now realised I was suffering a near nervous breakdown. On arrival in the camp John and I were allocated a bunk each in a room of twelve persons. One of the first meetings was in the cabin of the senior British officer. I found out later that the

Germans were in the habit of infiltrating the odd German person who might gain information. I was in such a state by this time that I could hardly speak to anyone and just wanted to burst into tears, symptoms of a nervous breakdown. Naturally I had not dared to tell John Worsley of my shooting the two Gestapo. This haunted me during the whole time in Marlag until the end of the war eighteen months later.

In our room each of us had a bunk, an upper or a lower, with bunk boards about ten inches wide. A mattress on top stuffed with wood shavings had the inevitable bed lice. After lights out, operated by the Germans, one person in the room spoke about his family life, wife or girlfriend. Luckily I think they realised I was in such a state that when my turn came to speak I was not expected to do so. After a few weeks we realised that familiarity breeds contempt and I vowed I would not reveal my private life. When I eventually became normal I varied my story each time it came round to my turn by, for example, saying I was a South African with a wife in Durban. Maybe a week or so later I said, 'You remember I told you about my wife in Durban, well I am not married and I had a very nice girlfriend there.' When they became a little annoyed, I said that I could not help noticing that people's intimate discussions bred contempt. From then on many of the roommates stopped relating their sexual prowess and other intimate aspects of their lives.

One of our roommates was a senior lieutenant in the Navy called Van Kerke, who spoke good German. He managed to get a daily copy of *Das Reich*, a German newspaper, and would tell us any news of interest. He was a submariner whose submarine had been depth-charged and sunk. Another was a warrant officer called John Willie Goble who was writing the story of his life, and when we asked him to let us see what he had written it sounded rather boring. He had been in the destroyer *Express*, blown up in a German minefield. Another was named Collinson, who did very little. The most interesting member of the room was Houston Rogers Smuts, as he had a beard like the South African General Smuts, and looked vaguely similar. He could play any instrument and was the head of the prisoners' camp band, was older than most of us and was universally liked. Another young member of the room, Lieutenant

Model making in the camp; a prisoner, believed to be Tony, working on a model boat. © IWM

The tools which Tony used to make Albert's eyes were supplied by the Germans through the Red Cross

Mewes, was christened Boy Mewes and spent much of his time walking round the camp perimeter. Finally there was an ex-Fleet Air Arm pilot whom we christened Lionel Strongfort, as his main hobby was keeping his muscles in trim and doing plenty of exercise.

During our time in Marlag many of the prisoners took up various hobbies. Mine were repairing watches and model-making. I still have the model yacht, designed by Collinson, which I built in the camp and which was returned to me by the Admiralty after the war. As wood was in short supply, I used planks from my bed boards for the hull, glued together one on top of another with UHU glue, and, following the plans, chipped away until I had achieved a rough outline. Finally, using templates, we achieved the exact shape of the outer hull before chiselling out the inside, again using a template. Eventually we had to bribe the guards for the essential parts of the boat, some lead for the keel, and the most important thing, a piece of wood for the hollow mast. This came from the camp commandant's garden, and had been a tomato plant support. Years later my son and daughter insisted on sailing it on a pond and it performed well.

6

AND ESCAPE AND RELIEF

Knowing I had an interest in watch repairing, the Swiss Red Cross donated a set of watchmaker's tools and an eyeglass to the camp and I was allowed to use a small room across the road from our hut to carry out repairs. As will be appreciated, there were a number of watch repairs for prisoners whose ships had been sunk and their watches ruined by salt water. The Red Cross was marvellous and supplied the camp with plenty of watch spares, and this occupied many hours of my time. One day we were advised that all prisoners were going to be inoculated against typhus and the Germans graciously supplied the camp doctor with five needles for over three hundred people. As can be imagined, the needles became blunt and the camp doctor asked if I would sharpen them on my watchmaker's sharpening stone, which I did, and then they were sterilised.

One day John Worsley, who was an extremely clever artist, said he could build a dummy that would fool the guards during the *Appell* or roll call that took place twice a day in the square. During each *Appell* we had to fall in hut by hut five ranks deep and be counted by one of the guards. If a prisoner happened to be ill they used to report 'Krank im Zimmer', and a guard would go to the relevant room and check that there was a sick man there. John started off by stuffing a pillowcase with straw and gradually shaping it into the rough outline of a head. He then cut strips of papier mâché which he glued to the embryo head and scraped away where necessary to maintain the shape. Eventually, when the desired head shape was achieved, he pulled out the straw, leaving a hollow papier mâché head. The next thing was to make the eyes from two ping-pong balls, with the eyelids carved from beech wood. Inside the hollow head he inserted a wire frame on which the eyeballs were fixed and I made the watch mechanism that gradually turned a balance wheel fitted with pins at irregular intervals. Whenever the dummy, nicknamed Albert, was moved and a pin came into the correct position it activated the eyelids. Albert now had a hollow head with eyes blinking at various intervals, but no body. A wire body frame was made that the head hooked on to and the trousers were in turn hooked on to the frame. Two prisoners in our room became Albert's handler and they spent hours walking up and down the corridor of the hut until they had the knack of being able to make Albert walk. When they were due to go out of the camp to the bath hut in the woods, the wire frames were concealed beneath their uniform and the head inside a bath towel. The day of the planned escape arrived and three prisoners in the room who had had nothing to do with carrying Albert tossed up as to who would go first. My turn came as No. 3 and the first two, who were friends, decided to go one after the other on the same day, meet up in the woods and head for Lübeck.

I had learnt to pick most locks and make keys to fit. As it was essential to open the lock into the toilet at the bathhouse, over a period of a month I made a key to fit. On arrival the escapee shut himself in the toilet. When the bath party returned to camp with the assembled Albert, he slipped out of the back window and hid in the woods. The next crocodile formed at the camp gates, again with the two handlers, but one of the guards said, 'You have just been for a shower! Aus!'

Near panic ensued and Albert's bits were passed to two other prisoners, who had never walked him before. All went well, with the bath party going through the routine and the second escapee hiding in the toilet. At the end of the shower the two new handlers assembled Albert and walked him between them to the assembly point in the yard. Unfortunately, having never handled Albert previously, they walked him with his feet slightly in the air and one of the guards, who had been an Austrian waiter and was very quick-witted, went up to Albert thinking he was drunk and shouted at him. No reply! He then

Albert RN

hit Albert with his rifle butt and the head fell off. Sadly, that was the end of Albert, who was re-assembled by the Germans and sent to the Berlin War Museum. The dummy was subsequently nicknamed Albert RN.

After the war John Worsley made another dummy for the film *Albert RN*, originally titled *Marlag O*, made in 1953. A replica dummy built by John in 1986 without blinking eyes is presently on show in the Royal Navy Museum at Portsmouth and another displayed at the RAF Escaping Society display in Lincolnshire. In 2009 I visited the Portsmouth naval museum to see John's dummy on display.

I also had an idea for an escape using a homemade hang-glider or kite built in our hut. The idea was for a number of us to run with a rope attached to the kite, while I hung on. We waited until there was a blackout during an air raid and ran the kite into wind. It became airborne with me but crashed almost immediately due to a lack of balance. I had forgotten the tail, the kite was written off, and I had a sore head.

One afternoon whilst I was walking round the camp perimeter, three of us were told to accompany the guard outside the camp. Suddenly we were back outside the Dulag where we had spent eight weeks in solitary confinement. We marched into a room where there were four or five other prisoners. Eventually I was taken to a nearby hut and into a room with other German army officers. Sitting between them at a desk was William Joyce, nicknamed Lord Haw-Haw, who used to broadcast from Germany saying, 'Germany calling, Germany calling' in a very distinctive nasal voice, and then talk a lot of nonsense. For example, 'The Forth Bridge was bombed and destroyed last night and it will take them a long time to build a fifth.' It soon turned out that he was trying to enlist people from among British and Allied prisoners to serve in the Blue Brigade and to fight on the Russian front. I recognised Haw-Haw from the big scar on his face, from when he was a follower of Sir Oswald Mosley, the British Fascist, and attended a rally in London. A heckler in the crowd threw a raw potato with a razor blade in it that hit Joyce on the cheek, causing the wound. During my interrogation I told the guards he was a traitor and that brought the interrogation to an end. We later returned to the camp and I am almost certain that Joyce got no recruits that day. Joyce was captured in 1945 and later hanged at Wandsworth Prison for treason.

As Christmas 1944 approached we decided to pool our cigarette allowance and purchase bottles of wine from the German guards who were sympathetic. Outside our room there was a small garden with a flowerbed and here we buried our supply of wine. Shortly before Christmas the weather turned extremely cold and everything froze solid. Van Kerke, with his excellent command of the German language, asked to see the camp commandant and told him that we were becoming very worried about the British terror *Flieger* (flyers). At the time the aerial activity over Germany was non-stop with the Americans bombing by day and the RAF by night. Van Kerke asked if we could have the loan of a pick and spade to dig a slit trench outside our hut. This was eventually provided and enabled us to dig our wine out of the frozen ground, the wine itself being frozen solid in the bottles. We cleaned the bottles and put them in a tin wash basin to melt the contents. We then threw the broken bits of the bottle away and drank a hotchpotch of mixed wine. Our liquid Christmas fare went down very well, and being unused to alcohol most of us had awful hangovers.

Sometimes we would have a concert and on one occasion a prisoner from Milag, which was the seamen's camp as opposed to the officers' camp, sent over Larry Adler, who played various tunes on his mouth organ, and we loved it. He became famous for his theme to the comedy film *Genevieve*.[32]

At the beginning of 1945 we all realised that the end of the war was fairly imminent as we had a homemade crystal set receiver that could pick up the BBC. We believed our German guards also realised that the war was about to change, and their attitude to the prisoners became far easier. A crude crystal set could be made from a coil made of salvaged wire, a rusty razor blade and a pencil lead for a diode. By lightly touching the pencil lead to spots of blue on the blade, or to spots of rust, they formed what is called a point contact diode and the rectified signal could be heard on headphones or crystal earpieces. Throughout my time the camp commandant was Schmidt, who had been a *Kapitän zur See* and was an old-style German naval officer, absolutely straight in the way he treated the prisoners and liked by everyone, unlike the Gestapo chief Goosevelt, who was an absolute sod. Towards April we heard gunfire in the distance and realised it was the advancing Allies. Orders were given to the camp guards that we should be marched away. We were ordered one morning to set off and could only take with us what we could carry. Most of the prisoners managed to make some sort of kitbag and it was soon realised by most of us that what we had decided to take with us would become very uncomfortable after a time. A friend of mine, a Royal Marines captain, had taken as many cigarettes as he could as a means of barter. When we passed through the first village he noticed a German woman with a pram. After quick negotiation he swapped the pram for cigarettes, which gave me a similar idea and we

51

set off with two prams full of our gear. We spent the nights in various woods, sometimes hot and sometimes very cold. About four days into the march many columns of marching men were being strafed by Allied aircraft.

One morning American Thunderbolt aircraft were sighted and peeled off heading for our column. I dived into a ditch and bullets splintered the tree above me, with bits of wood raining down like hail. Sadly, a senior British officer who stood up to wave at the aircraft was shot to pieces. On another night we were in a barn when the whine of aircraft engines grew louder and louder. We felt sure they were attacking us. However, they passed over and pulled away and it was later found that a German column had been attacked.

We eventually arrived at Lübeck on 23 April and were put in a virtually unguarded camp with a number of Polish prisoners. On the second day the Poles decided to give a concert and we all stood in the main open space of the camp. Two Poles, one with a piano accordion, played 'Jealousy' and sang in Polish. They performed so beautifully that we all had tears in our eyes. The following day a British armoured division overran us and a British major in a Bren carrier arrived at the camp gates and asked if any action by our guards went against the Geneva Convention. We all pointed at Goosevelt, who had crept up on prisoners treading in the forbidden raked area by the fence and one evening shot one of them. Having been overrun, the guards, including Goosevelt, had packed all their bags and were sitting in their cars, hopefully ready to go home. The major in the Bren carrier said to Goosevelt, 'Come here!' in a loud voice. Goosevelt tried to ignore it until the major's order was repeated in a loud voice and Goosevelt slowly walked across. The major said, 'Take your boots off', and on the second order he did and was then told, 'Run!' As he started to run he was shot. Schoof, however, was nowhere to be found as he had been clever enough to slip away.[33] Into the camp came another naval officer in a staff car who had been in the commandos with me. He told me to get in and shortly afterwards we drove off in the direction of Lüneburg. The German countryside was in a terrible state with dead cows and sheep lying rigid on their backs all over the place. We finally arrived at an RAF station near Lüneburg and found that an ENSA concert had just finished.[34] He and I went to the bar, and were surrounded by some very pretty girls and plied with drinks. This was a bad thing because I was very thin, just under eight stone, and apart from our Christmas bash had not tasted any alcohol for some time. I eventually bedded down under a billiard table with the most monumental hangover.

Early next morning I was wakened by the sound of aircraft followed by gunfire. It transpired that a flight of German aircraft had come over to surrender and Johnnie Johnson, one of our fighter aces based at Lüneburg, scrambled his men and shot them down.[35] I then split from my rescuer, who had other work to do, and thumbed a lift in a Dakota as far as Brussels. Things were pretty chaotic and I wandered across the tarmac to see another Dakota with its door still open but about to take off for England. I managed to climb aboard and landed at Biggin Hill, where I thumbed a lift on a lorry to Victoria Station. I stopped the first naval officer I could see and said, 'Look, I am terribly sorry, I have just come out of a German prisoner-of-war camp, could you lend me a pound?' He took a look at me and said, 'I can see you have, have this on me, you don't have to pay me back.' I caught a tube train and an old lady plucked my sleeve and said, 'Doesn't anybody look after you?' It was only then I realised how dishevelled I was.

Having arrived at Waterloo, I bought a ticket to Guildford and telephoned the Weatherill family who had been the next-door neighbours to my aunts' flat in Guildford. My girlfriend, a Weatherill daughter, met me at Guildford station and we drove in her father's car back to their house. On arrival the family suggested the first thing I should do was have a bath, after which Bernard Weatherill, often known as Jack, who later became the Speaker of the House of Commons, advised me to drain the water and run another. This I did and only then realised that I had lice in my hair and I must have smelt rather ghastly.

Next morning, 6 June 1945, I borrowed a suit from Jack and took the train to London. I went to Piccadilly and had a haircut and had my beard, which I had had for the past year, shaved off. I must say my face felt very cold without a beard. Walking up Piccadilly, I arrived at Gieves the outfitters who made naval officers' uniforms. I asked one of the assistants if I could be measured for a new reefer jacket. 'Excuse me, sir', he said, 'are you an ex-prisoner of war?' When I said that I was he said, 'Just a moment', disappeared, and came back with a brand-new uniform. All naval prisoners were given a new uniform courtesy of Gieves. I went into the fitting room and put the reefer on, which went almost twice around me – the trousers were likewise too large. They were duly altered and I reported to the Admiralty at Queen Anne's Mansions, gave them the Weatherills' address, and was told to go on twenty-one days' leave until further orders.

Obviously all ex-prisoners were very run down and within a week I caught measles and poor Mrs Weatherill nursed me back to health.

7

CHANGING COURSE

O n 26 June 1945 I was summoned by the Admiralty and told
that all ex-prisoner Royal Naval Officers had to go on courses
to be brought up to date with the latest naval procedures. At
the end of the war the Admiralty combined navigation and fighter
direction, and instead of being purely a ship's navigator with a cubby-
hole to oneself, the navigator might be one of five fighter direction and
navigation officers in a large ship. This did not suit me at all and so I
asked if I could join the Fleet Air Arm as a pilot, and was sent on an
elementary flying training course at RAF Clyffe Pypard near Swindon,
where we were taught in Tiger Moths.

At this point I think it is worth explaining the reason why I learnt
to fly. I had always been very interested in navigation and in the various
ships managed to become an assistant to the Navigation Officer and
after a time was trusted enough to take sights and work out a position.
The only accurate way is by taking star sights with a sextant. The best
way to plot one position is through a sun sight. A noon sight always
gives the altitude position, which is called a meridian altitude and is
the moment the sun is due north. The time is worked out when the sun
will be highest around noon. The sextant is set about fifteen minutes
before the meridian altitude and is constantly checked until the sun
starts to decrease, having just passed its highest point, which gives an
accurate altitude. I managed to acquire a star globe and picked out at
least four stars at various bearings in the sky. Ideally these would be
four stars bearing ninety degrees from each other, but this was never

possible. The star globe is set up and the earliest time after sunset the stars will come into view is calculated, starting with the strongest star, namely Sirius. Having noted each star's altitude and bearing in the notebook, the sky is swept with the sextant until, for example, Sirius comes into view. Ideally one should have an assistant with notebook and the deck watch, where one sweeps the sky, adjusting the sextant, so the arc just touches the horizon. The order is given, 'Stand by, stop!' the moment an accurate reading has been taken of the star cutting the horizon, and the assistant notes the time, a rough bearing of the star and the sextant reading. After this has been done and sights have been taken of all the stars, an estimated position is then worked out on a plotting diagram. If the estimated position were the actual position, the intercepts from each star would cross each other exactly at the position calculated. When I was plotting on the chart table, sometimes the captain would come into the room and watch the work. This was very off-putting. I tried not to rub out my previous day's calculations and the captain soon got the message.

RAF Clyffe Pypard had a grass runway and a number of large hangars for the aircraft. The Tiger Moth is a single-engine biplane in which the instructor sits in the front cockpit and the pupil in the rear. We carried out circuits and bumps. Initially the bumps were indeed that, until after a few hours we learnt how to make a smooth landing. We came into land over the perimeter fence at about 50 mph, throttle right back, and glided into land. Eventually, after about eight hours of dual flying, the instructor got out of the aircraft and pupils were sent off on their first solo flight. This involved a take-off, a circuit, and a landing. After a number of solo flights we were sent off on a cross-country trip and there was another area for aerobatics. I went solo on 11 February 1946 after fifteen hours' dual instruction.

An amusing interlude occurred one day when my instructor informed me he was going to accompany me. We went off towards an area where the father of one of the pupils had a farm. Having taken off, the instructor said, 'I have got her', and followed another pupil who had gone off across country. To the instructor's horror and my amusement, we saw a Tiger Moth take off from a field, with the pupil pilot in full flying uniform standing at the edge of the field and his aircraft taking off with an unknown person in the cockpit. My instructor landed in the field, switched off the engine, climbed out and went up to the other pupil standing in his flying kit. The pupil came up and said, 'It is all right, sir; it's Dad on his first solo.' Evidently he had trained his father, who had been in the RAF during the war, to brush up his flying skills. I never found out what the punishment was.

After a specified number of hours, the elementary flying training was complete and pupils were given their wings. This was followed by an Advanced Flying Training Course at Yeovilton.

By the beginning of June 1946 I had become very unsettled in the Navy. All ex-prisoners of war were given the option of leaving the service, and having opted to leave, I sat before a panel of doctors and gave my reasons. We were told how much it had cost to train officers to that level. Whilst I did not know what I would do, I was adamant I wanted to leave and on 23 September my resignation was accepted. I was given a demobilisation suit, which was ghastly, and, as I had been a regular naval officer, I had to pay the princely sum of £54. I left the service in October 1946.

I regained contact with Dick Bainbridge, with whom I had sailed

home from Durban four years before, thanks to a naval doctor, Don Stewart, who knew Dick, and I went to stay with him and his sister Kiddo at their cottage in Yateley. Dick had a garage at Blackwater, near Camberley, specialising in pre-war Bentleys. We used to leave the cottage in our various old cars and change into overalls at the garage, where I manned the petrol pump, occasionally being given a tip by a customer. Kiddo owned an old ketch named *Orestes*, built at

Tony and Kiddo aboard Orestes

Oreston near Plymouth, which originally used to carry cargoes of fruit and nuts from Spain to Plymouth. Kiddo had married Jim Stead just before the war and *Orestes* was his yacht converted from the old fruit and nut clipper. Sadly, Jim had been killed in the Navy near Tobruk and *Orestes* spent the war on a mud berth up the Bag at Salcombe. When I first went with them to see her, she was in a sorry state. The mizzenmast had rotted and collapsed, and the topsides had gaps between the planking where the caulking had opened.

I was full of hope in those days and Dick and I set about getting the old vessel seaworthy. The topside planks were kept in position with tunnels, or treenails, whereby a round peg with a small slit in either end was hammered into the planking and the frame, then a small wedge of wood was knocked in to expand the end. We found some of the frames were rotten and scarfed in new pieces. Looking back, I don't know how we thought we could repair her but somehow we did. We bought a new length of wood, which was adzed to shape for the mizzenmast, and gradually the old ship came together again. After many visits to Salcombe, the great day arrived when we put to sea and sailed her to the Hamble River, where she was berthed at Solent Shipyard. The hull was painted with black and white gunports and had a 28-foot bowsprit and figurehead.

In Solent Shipyard we acquired another piece of silver spruce and shaped it into a square yard. When at last she was completed she had an inner and outer jib, a square sail, main and topsail and a mizzen. *Orestes* was finally ready for sea in 1947 and Dick put together a crew consisting of Kiddo, Donald McCormack, John Tudor-Owen, who had been at Ampleforth with me, and myself. Donald had been a torpedo officer in the war and was one of the nicest men you could meet, but he was cack-handed. For example, he borrowed my 1923 30/98 Vauxhall car whilst we were at the shipyard and hit the kerb, resulting in a puncture.

We agreed to sail *Orestes* to South Africa and at the last moment Box, my father, arrived from Ceylon and asked to come with us for the first part of the journey to the Mediterranean. *Orestes* was given customs clearance and we departed on 14 August 1947. Luckily the weather was calm with little wind and the ship had an easy passage across the Bay of Biscay. Dick decided to put into Vigo, our first foreign port. I was navigator and had taken a sight about a hundred miles short of Vigo when thick fog came down and we slowed as a result. The next morning a dead-reckoning position put us off the Portuguese coast some twenty miles from Vigo and we altered course to the east and crept in to make landfall. Luckily the fog cleared and our dead-reckoning position had been accurate, and we made Vigo that afternoon. A fiesta was taking place accompanied by a lot of music, and we went ashore for our first foreign dinner.

From Vigo we sailed slowly down the Spanish coast, past Lisbon, to our next port of call, Cadiz. On arrival everything was closed, as Manolete, the principal bullfighter at the time, had been badly gored a few days previously and died just before our arrival.[36] From Cadiz we headed for Gibraltar and berthed off the yacht club. Dick decided a considerable amount of work needed to be done on the ship and we stayed for about six weeks. One day the posters in Gibraltar advertised an afternoon bullfight at a building in La Linea. With the exception of Kiddo, who declined, we went ashore and had a liquid lunch at a small restaurant near the bullring. After lunch we found the bullfight was not until five and Box decided that we must have some Egyptian PT.[37] He made sounds to the waiter that we wanted a siesta and also made a sign of sleeping. A waiter appeared who spoke English and Box again said he wanted to sleep. The waiter seemed a little embarrassed and said, 'Señor, no women are available until six.'

However, we stayed in the restaurant and had a siesta at the table. We obtained good seats at the bullfight but it was not to our taste and we left after the fight, feeling it was a very cruel spectacle. The next morning we sailed into the Mediterranean and arrived at Majorca where we stocked up with several demijohns of Spanish wine and sherry. When Dick went to pay the bill we were told that it was very cheap as none of it had been declared. We went into panic stations, cast off and sailed within half an hour, stowing demijohns as we left.

A further member of the crew was Kiddo's Alsatian, William. Strangely, apart from his mistress, I was the only person who could control William. He slept on a starboard settee in the main cabin and at sea a small coil of rope was put up forward on deck on which William did the necessary. It was then trawled astern until thoroughly clean.

We arrived in Malta in November 1947 and my father left the ship to return to England prior to returning to Ceylon. It was getting cold in England at that time of year so I gave him my naval greatcoat. A few days after my father had left, there appeared on board a Frenchman named J. J. Tremayne who had served in the Royal Navy during the war and had taken part in several operations in France, eventually gaining British citizenship. JJ asked to join the crew and opted to sleep on the starboard bunk in the saloon. William disliked the arrangement and frequently whilst in Malta, when JJ came aboard fairly late, he found William sleeping on his bunk. In his French accent we would hear him plead, 'Good William, please get off my bunk.' The reply was always a growl from William and further French swear words from JJ, until Kiddo came out of her cabin and took William into it.[38]

Orestes was berthed in Sliema creek and we rigged a rubber dinghy on a rope and tackle between the quay and the gangway. A considerable amount of further work was carried out on the ship and eventually we sailed just after Christmas for Port Said. The only local weather report we obtained predicted an impending gale and two days after sailing we ran into terrible weather. Luckily this was a following gale, though it turned out to be the worst storm for several years in the Mediterranean. The square yard had been stowed on deck before leaving Malta and we lashed a tarpaulin to it and streamed it out on two lines astern. With the ship under bare poles, frequent pumping of the bilges was necessary. The gale was so bad that when the two watchkeepers were on deck they had to shout at each other to be heard, and for a time we were uncertain if we would make it. After several days the storm gradually abated and we were able to bend on the mainsail and mizzen. Eventually we sighted the lights of Port Said and hove to until daylight. On entering the port we anchored across from Simon Artz with its Johnnie Walker sign, 'Still going strong'.[39] The port authorities were horrified when we said we wanted to transit the Suez Canal. We were obliged to take a canal pilot and told to maintain a speed of about 7 knots. This was impossible out of the old diesel, although we promised to do so. On entering the canal, the pilot kept saying 'More speed, more speed.' Dick said we could do this by setting some sail but this idea didn't appeal to the pilot. A fairly stiff drink pacified him, in spite of his faith, and gradually we piled on more sail until we reached the Bitter Lakes under full sail at the required 7 knots. Ultimately we arrived at the end of the canal with no further incidents and the pilot was so happy to get off that Kiddo received a big kiss from him.

We had a following wind south of Suez and eventually even had the square sail up. According to the Red Sea pilot, a northerly wind at this time of year petered out by Port Sudan, and by Perim Island we would meet the strong southerly wind. The great thing in those days was that the map everywhere was printed in red for British territories and independence was still a thing of the future. Sure enough, the wind petered out the further south we sailed and in due course we arrived at Massawa in Ethiopia, still controlled by the British. We were advised that the best way for a sailing vessel to get through the Perim Straits to Aden was to sail late in the afternoon and put in behind one of the islands before the wind got up in the morning. We sailed for the Dahlak Islands and a local dhow captain confirmed that the only way they traded up and down the coast was to sail at night and lay up in the lee of an island at dawn. We gradually edged our way south, anchoring in the lee of various islands and taking it in turns to keep anchor watch.

One night Donald woke me for my watch and said he had caught several fish, including a shark. On inspection his shark measured about nine inches, but the fish made good eating. The next night my watch ended at midnight and I did not wake up until about 6 a.m., by which time we had passed through the Straits of Perim and set course for Aden. After loading minimum supplies we sailed the next day. We had read in *The Africa Pilot* that the best way to sail south was to go as far as Socotra and The Brothers,[40] and set course about 200 miles off the East African coast where we would meet a counter-current. This we were able to achieve and had a fair and easy passage towards Mombasa. On our final day as we approached the East African coast we felt the north-going current had already set in, and entered Mombasa twenty-three days after leaving Aden.

Above: Orestes *at sea* Below: *The* Orestes *figurehead*

8

EAST AFRICA

At Mombasa a pilot came aboard and showed us the best spot to anchor. We dropped the anchor and set a stern line to a buoy in the harbour, the harbour being sheltered from the main channel. This became our permanent mooring and enabled us to go ashore easily. Our passage down the coast heralded the end of the monsoon and for the poor old *Orestes* it was obvious that we could no longer go south until a further six months had elapsed. It had been suggested that we look up Eileen Jolly, whose husband had taken her to stay temporarily at Shelly Beach Hotel, on the south side of Mombasa Island, and we decided to walk round one afternoon. Sadly, Stratford J, Eileen's husband who had been a great explorer before the war, had died at the hotel and Eileen, who was not lacking in the ready, bought the hotel. At the same time Dick decided to go to Durban to look up his old wartime girlfriend, and we received a cable three weeks later saying 'Married Charmaine yesterday.' John Tudor-Owen left us for a job and J. J. Tremayne also signed off and went his own way.

Kiddo, Donald and I, with William the dog, were the only ones left on board. Kiddo took William to Shelly Beach Hotel, as Eileen believed there was much more scope for William ashore than on board the yacht. William was just over eighteen years old and, sadly, two weeks later he collapsed chasing a land crab on the beach and died that evening. Dick arrived back a fortnight later with his pretty new wife, but both Kiddo and I realised we were likely to have many problems with her. Charmaine decided that life on board a yacht was not for her and made Dick move ashore to a small local hotel, The Moorings, then later to a thatched banda (beach hut) down the coast near Shelly Beach Hotel. Box, my father, then invited Kiddo and me to visit Ceylon and stay with him. After a trip on the Bank Line ship *Isipingo*, we were met by Box and his motor fishing vessel (MFV) which was looked after by his Sinhalese coxswain. Box very generously gave me the boat, after previously telling me that he was having trouble with her. I replied that he did not know how to look after her and was immediately told to see what I could do with her. I went aboard with the coxswain and galley boy and before long set off for East Africa.

After eighteen days we arrived in Mombasa and found that the Fisheries Department was looking for an MFV. The next day I concluded a deal and sold her for £5,000. Whilst I had been in Ceylon, Box told me that the Admiralty had sunk a number of these craft at Trincomalee at the end of the war as there was no further use for them. I immediately contacted Dick. He and I and Charmaine set off on the next Bank Line ship, richer by my £5,000, and returned to Trincomalee.

Dick also added £5,000 from the sale of his Knightsbridge building. There was a very nice club, the Sea Anglers, where we bought a 45-foot MFV in running order, and three others under water, for which we paid £200 to the Canteen Fund of the Naval Dockyard. We also hired the Coastal Forces Slipway, near the club, for the princely sum of one rupee a day. We found out that in the pettah (native quarter) in Colombo there was a store owned by some Sinhalese merchants called Mabel Stores, which was a goldmine of ex-Navy spares, including diesel engines and every conceivable type of stores that we required.

Charmaine, who by now was pregnant, left for Colombo to have the baby delivered by Dr Victor Dowse, an old family friend. A baby girl was born and christened Jane, who became my first goddaughter and took up residence with us at the Sea Anglers Club.

By diving and closing the open valves, we raised the first two MFVs and re-engined them from the pettah. Donald and I decided to sail them to Mombasa with me as navigator, and Donald, who was an excellent cook, guaranteed me a daily lunch. We set off in convoy, stopping en route in the Maldive Islands. We serviced the engines once a day, checking the oil and so on. One of my deck boys would take over the helm and steer on a parallel course to Donald's and as we came alongside I would jump across, service Donald's engine and have a slap-up lunch with him. After lunch my MFV came alongside and I would jump across again. There was a certain amount of danger involved as due to the ocean swell both these small craft used to roll and we could not get too near in case the craft knocked against each other. Sometimes I would ask for my craft to come round again until sufficiently close for me to jump over and grab the guardrails.

The other problem on these small craft was cockroaches. They seemed to multiply almost overnight. Some were large –we named them Bombay Canaries and I occasionally woke up in my bunk, put the light on, and found a large one standing on my chest. To catch them the procedure was to fill a jar containing a little ground-up coffee and leave it out overnight. By the morning there was frequently a trail of cockroaches crawling up the sides of the jar and into a black mass inside. One of us put our hand on top of the jar and then threw them over the side.

When we arrived in Mombasa, both MFVs were anchored across Kilindini harbour, and Donald had to leave for his job with the Agricultural Department in Shinyanga in Tanganyika (now Tanzania). I went back to Trincomalee and the Sea Anglers Club where Dick had acquired yet another MFV, a 75-footer with a huge diesel engine and a marvellous winch on the foredeck, belt driven from the engine room. The only drawback was that the engine was in little pieces all over the engine room and the Sinhalese owners were unable to reassemble it. It took Dick, a born but unqualified engineer, a considerable time to reassemble everything. We also became very friendly with two naval officers from the dockyard, one of whom was an engineer. Over a period Dick persuaded Chimp Woods, the engineer, that a very nice lathe they had was surplus to requirements, and he had it moved over to us on loan. Eventually Chimp Woods found it was no longer on the books in the dockyard and thereafter it belonged to us.

Lying in Trinco was very pleasant. One of our pastimes was catching crayfish and I worked out a way of taking them alive. Round

Sober Island there were many crayfish which came into shallow water at night. Whilst they were being speared we noticed that if we missed, they would kick backwards at great speed before turning and swimming to deep water. I soldered an old car headlamp to make it watertight and stuck a hollow brass tube on to the back of the headlight, complete with electric wires attached to a 12-volt battery. One of us would row the dinghy stern first with the headlamp floating over the stern and swivelled from side to side looking for our prey. We made a net with a wire loop on a handle to catch the crayfish and heave it into the dinghy. As we had noticed, a near miss made the crayfish do a violent movement astern or backwards. The first time we tried out our new equipment we hit the jackpot. As we shone the light on the deeper side of the water the crayfish would gently start walking up to the shallow water. Having manoeuvred the crayfish, we would gently lower the net to the bottom behind the crayfish and give a quick stab with the end of an oar in front of them. The crayfish would take violent action rearwards and into the net, the bottom of which was sealed. On our first attempt we caught nine crayfish and then had to stop as they were crawling around the bottom of the dinghy, making it necessary to keep our feet clear of their spiny feelers.

Ceylon had very little rise and fall in tide and the maximum at spring tides was three feet. We made a wire pen on the beach of the club with rocks under which the crayfish could hide and we fed them bits of rotten fish each day. Box used to come and go from the Sea Anglers Club to his tea estate at Dalhousie, one of the highest in Ceylon. The estate house was beautifully built with leaded windows and parquet floors, and had a large attractive garden. In this garden the previous owner had planted orchids, as a hobby. One day we decided to count the types of orchids and estimated that there were forty-five different types in the trees. Every morning the servants placed a bowl of fresh orchids in the drawing room and these were changed each day. When I suggested to the head boy that it was quite unnecessary to do this every day, the reply was, 'Master says fresh orchids every day.' So there it was.

The road from Colombo up to the estate at Maskeliya continued into a track on the edge of the estate to Adam's Peak, which had a Buddhist shrine. Box had built a small cabin where hot drinks could be given to the many pilgrims who passed through the edge of the estate. This was a good move, because nothing was ever stolen. Back at the Sea Anglers Club we noticed that one of our raised 50-foot MFVs had obviously been better built and we decided to give it back to Box in return for his kindness to me in giving me his original MFV. We purchased a new diesel engine at Mabel Stores and took over Box's estate carpenter, who built a fine cabin aft of the wheelhouse that he could use as a sleeping cabin. Box was lonely on his own on the estate since my mother's tragic death in 1938 and a different person when he was with us, and was always getting offers for the Dalhousie estate. He had remarried, but the woman had an eye for the main chance and absconded with the substantial family silver. Dick persuaded him to accept a very good offer and join us all when we finally went back to East Africa.

The day arrived when the 75-foot MFV, which we had renamed *Southern Cross*, was ready for engine trials and when Dick started her up she ran like new. We decided that she was powerful enough to tow the two other small MFVs astern and for Box to keep company with us in his own MFV. Towing two craft astern meant having a long towline

Southern Cross

67

with a heavy anchor in the middle of the towline to stop it coming up taut. We eventually set off via the Maldives for Addu Atoll. Each evening Box would roar past us in his faster MFV and we would hold up a large blackboard giving him the course for the night. He and his couple of crew would take the wheel and take station about 200 yards on our beam. This worked well but one night Dick woke me during his watch saying that Box had gradually increased speed and was about to disappear over the horizon ahead of us. We both agreed that it would be fatal to lose him and Dick believed we would have to let go the tow to rescue him. Once the tow was freed, with a heavy anchor between the two small MFVs, they would eventually smash together and it would be quite impossible for us to pick up the tow again. I agreed with Dick that we should wait another twenty minutes before slipping the anchor. Happily, Box had woken up, decided to go out on deck to spend a penny and was horrified to find we had disappeared. As it turned out, his coxswain had inadvertently nudged the throttle which resulted in the increased speed. The sky ahead was suddenly lit up with flares and thank God he stopped. We were able to catch up with him. Two days later we arrived at Addu Atoll lagoon, where we were able to anchor in a depth of water that allowed the anchors of the two small MFVs to hit the bottom, thus enabling them to remain apart. We put Box into the tow to stop any further problems. After a few days at Addu Atoll, we set sail for the Seychelles and in the evening we would pass a fishing line with food to him as his cook was utterly useless and ours produced some excellent food.

We arrived in the Seychelles and anchored in Mahé. The main hotel, a wooden structure on the quay, was called the Imperial and was run by a Mrs Whiterite. When we came to sail for Mombasa, Box decided he would stay in the Seychelles on his MFV and eat at the hotel. A few weeks later, having arrived in Mombasa, I received a letter from Box bemoaning the fact that the food at the Imperial was the same every day. I wrote back, 'If you do not like it, why don't you buy the hotel?', which he promptly did and dismissed Mrs Whiterite. Box renamed the hotel the Pirate's Arms and turned many of the rooms into suites. I received a letter some months later complaining the hotel was losing money. He had written to all his friends asking them to come and stay, which they did without paying. Box was so kind-hearted, he would not dream of charging them.[41]

On arrival in Mombasa we sold one of the towed MFVs and chartered the other. With the *Southern Cross*, Dick and I realised we must trade her along the coast to try and make some money. There was a small company in Kilindini Road called Lewis & Paton. Crash Lewis, the senior partner, had previously had a small vessel of his own and persuaded Dick that there was good money to be made in the Comoros purchasing vanilla beans and bringing them back to East Africa to sell. He suggested to Dick they should take the *Southern Cross* and split the proceeds 50/50. There was also good money to be made in carrying Comoran passengers from Zanzibar to Moroni.[42] I saw them off at Zanzibar and returned to Mombasa to join Kiddo on *Orestes*. Donald had written from Shinyanga asking us to go and stay with him in his tented camp. Kiddo and I travelled by train from Dar es Salaam in Tanganyika and had a rattly journey to Shinyanga, where a man called Williamson had just discovered diamonds and set up a business which later became world-famous as the Williamson Diamond Mines (also known as the Mwadui mine). Donald took us to see the District Officer, a friend of his, who opened his desk and showed us fifty or more uncut diamonds smuggled out by locals. We went off in Donald's truck to his camp in the bush about twenty miles away. There were two tents, one for Kiddo and the other shared by Donald and me. Donald as usual fed himself extremely well, with game he shot himself. One night I was knocked out of bed when a rhino lumbered through, taking our tent and continuing on his way, the remains of the tent being found about 200 yards away. Luckily our beds had not been broken and Donald had a spare tent. In those days the surrounding bundu (jungle) was very primitive and we used to go for long walks with a rifle each, as there was considerable wildlife.

Kiddo and I eventually returned to Mombasa to find Dick's trip had been a complete financial disaster. Unbeknown to us, Crash Lewis had in the past smuggled a great deal of vanilla and the French authorities in the Comoros would have nothing to do with him. The partnership he had suggested between us was immediately dissolved and we set up our own headquarters in Zanzibar. Another trade during the northeast monsoon was from Zanzibar to Pemba, with clove pickers as passengers and a cargo of cloves on the return. For this short trip the *Southern Cross* was certified to carry 100 deck passengers and it was non-stop – up with passengers, load the hold with bags of cloves, take clove pickers back on board, and back to Zanzibar.

I decided to take the *Southern Cross* to the Comoros, having been told the items to take were kangas (colourful African printed garments) and rubber sandals. I bought cratefuls from Smith Mackenzie's in Mombasa and set off for Moroni. As I spoke good French I was allowed by the authorities to sell all my goods in customs and buy goods for Zanzibar. Prior to leaving, a Chinaman in Zanzibar had said that he would purchase sharks' fins and an Indian merchant was in the market for bales of coir yarn made from coconut husk fibre. The coir yarn came from Dzaoudzi and I struck a deal with the Indian merchant for a fairly large consignment. This was sold by weight and the merchant had his scales in his godown (warehouse). After having carefully weighed and loaded the cargo, we set off for Zanzibar. Here the Chinaman arrived for his sharks' fins, packed in sacks, and as they were emptied he said, 'No good, no good, no good, all right.' This went on until he had bought all he wanted, which was less than a quarter of what I had. He explained there was only one type of shark's fin they used, which I noted for the future. Next the Asian came to weigh the coir yarn, which was about half the weight that I had paid for in the Comoros godown. The Asian explained to me that all Indian merchants liked to sell coir yarn in godowns where it was liberally sprinkled with water. In future I should stipulate that I would only buy it open on the quay.

On the next trip I insisted that the coir seller would have it on the quay and I told him that as I was in a hurry he must have it out by 9 o'clock in the morning. The nahoda (captain) on the *Southern Cross*, also a Comoran, said he would keep an eye on the coir. Again we stipulated 9 o'clock and the cargo was duly lined up on the quay, being guarded by my nahoda. The seller kept asking where I was and around midday we decided it would be dry enough to load. Needless to say, my nahoda watered it liberally on the trip over to Zanzibar and we made a good profit.

It was here in the Comoros that the first coelacanth fish had been found. At that time Professor Smith, a South African, had a very rotten fish brought to him that he identified as a coelacanth. He left posters to be put in the saloons of various passenger liners coming up from South Africa as far as Mombasa, offering a reward of £100 for any information on a coelacanth. It was known that the fish lived at a great depth. Eric Hunt, who lived in Zanzibar, chartered one of our 50-foot MFVs, which we had towed over from Trincomalee. Eric had met Professor Smith and kept a small stock of formalin on his MFV, being the eternal optimist.[43] Eric mentioned that, in the market at Moroni and on the island of Anjouan, the locals used a very large and abrasive fish scale for rubbing on bicycle inner tubes when mending a puncture. On his next trip Eric took dozens of leaflets showing a picture of a coelacanth and offering £100 reward, which he distributed round the fish markets in Moroni and the other islands of the Comoros. During one of his trips he was loading coir yarn at Anjouan and was due to have lunch with the French governor. The previous day over the mountain from the capital, Mutsamudu, a local schoolmaster was talking to two fishermen who were about to cut up a very large and ugly fish they considered would have no takers. The schoolmaster said he thought this looked very like the fish that bwana Hunt was looking for, and so they took it over the mountain to Eric's MFV in the harbour. Eric was about to start lunch with the governor, when his Comoran bo'sun arrived and whispered to him, 'Bwana, your fish has arrived.' Eric left the lunch party as soon as he could, went aboard the boat and, lo and behold, there was a coelacanth in the hold. Eric immediately injected it with formalin and sailed for the island of Mayotte. He sent a cable to Professor Smith that went via Tananarive in Madagascar. On its arrival Professor Smith obtained permission from the South African government to fly to Mayotte with a South African Air Force crew in a Dakota DC3. It appears that Tananarive had not advised the French government, as it was Christmas. Professor Smith immediately identified the fish from Mayotte as a coelacanth and a photograph was taken of Eric, Professor Smith and the South African Air Force crew with the coelacanth. The fish was duly flown back in the DC3 and the story published in the South African newspapers. It was subsequently put on display in the aquarium on the waterfront in Cape Town.

The French government was furious. The upshot was that all French government employees in Madagascar and the Comoros were investigated and those who had been Vichy employees were dismissed. Since then several coelacanths have been caught by various expeditions but none were alive. Because they live in very deep water their bodies burst when they come to the surface. Shortly after this Eric Hunt went to Europe and bought a schooner for himself. Eric was not a very good navigator and the furthest south he went was Majunga in Madagascar. On a trip between Madagascar and the Comoros he missed the islands and grounded on a coral reef. He set sail towards East Africa in the schooner's dinghy with the bo'sun but after several weeks Eric died and the emaciated bo'sun was the sole survivor.[44]

9

BUSINESS GROWS

By 1952 Dick and I had around £10,000 in the bank and we decided that we should branch out and purchase a Dutch steel coaster. I flew to Holland, found a local shipbroker and negotiated for a small 200-ton coaster. There appeared to be another broker involved called Westera, who lived in Zwolle. During my time as a guest of the Führer I had learnt quite a lot of German; in Zwolle they speak a form of Plattdeutsch or Low German and while my broker was in contact with Westera I realised that I was being overcharged. I had a row with the broker and went on to England. It had been suggested that I get in touch with H. E. Moss & Co., shipbrokers in the city of London, whose chairman was Richard Favell, an ex-naval officer who was also a partner with his uncle in Moss Tankers. I explained the position to him and through H. E. Moss they negotiated the purchase of the Dutch coaster at its true price of £9,000. Richard and his wife Barbara became great friends and I used to stay with them at Woking. We used Moss for all our purchases and sales until I sold Southern Line and Mahé Shipping.

The vessel was renamed *Southern Trader* and handed over to me at Boston, Lincolnshire, after she had discharged her cargo. She then sailed for Shadwell Basin in London, where I obtained a full cargo of wines and spirits from Saccone & Speed for Mombasa. When the stevedores appeared to load the vessel I spoke to one of the foremen and explained to him that this was my little ship and to give me a fair run. He turned round to all the stevedores who were going down into the hold and said, 'This chap is trying to make his own living so

Tony beside the Southern Trader, London *prior to departure for Mombasa*

look after it.' It was remarkable that when we arrived in East Africa there was no loss whatsoever on the cargo. On arrival in Aden I took a small additional amount of deck cargo and set off for Ras Hafun, a headland off Somalia. We hit some very nasty weather and eventually anchored under the lee of the headland. The water temperature on the north side of Ras Hafun was bitterly cold and the *East African Pilot* states that the north-going current hits the south of Ras Hafun and is deflected eastward and generates a counter-current further out to sea. This obviously was responsible for the drop in temperature in our anchorage. On our first evening I took the dinghy with a couple of the crew and found a mass of crayfish in the shallows. We had an excellent dinner and lay there for several days awaiting a change in the weather. I had been advised that the best way down the Somalia coast was to stay inside the 100-fathom mark, hug the coast and stay in sight of it the whole time. The passage to Mogadishu was laborious, necessitating me staying on deck all night keeping an eye on the coast and eventually handing over to a helmsman during daylight hours. We reached Mogadishu and carried on to Mombasa's old port.

At the time there was such congestion in Mombasa's Kilindini port that ships were often held up offloading for three to four weeks. However, I took the cargo into the old port, where there was no delay.

The big companies who were agents for the East African Conference Lines lodged a protest with the government that I should not be allowed to discharge in the old port. This of course was turned down and we later received a very nice letter from Saccone & Speed that they had never had a delivery before without breakage or pilferage.

One of the early salvage jobs we took on was the converted steam trawler *Derna*, which ran up and down the coast carrying a small general cargo. On 21 July 1954 the ship grounded on Niule Reef outside Tanga while entering the port with a cargo of 400 drums of petrol. A week later the cargo had been recovered by floating the drums ashore and the ship abandoned with a flooded engine room. A salvage team headed by myself arrived, having signed a Lloyd's Open Form on a no cure, no pay basis, and set about refloating the vessel 200 yards from the sea at low water.[45] After patching the leaks and pumping, the vessel was nearly afloat on the high tide. Using two heavy anchors as ground tackle and wires from the *Southern Cross* wrapped around the *Derna*'s superstructure, she was slowly hauled off the reef. On 27 August the ship refloated and was towed via Tanga to Mombasa. Two weeks later, while anchored in Mtongwe, the *Derna* sank in unexplained circumstances, leaving the funnel and mast tops above the surface. The age of the vessel and extent of repairs required after the grounding meant further salvage operations were abandoned and the ship was left where she still is today.

The steam trawler Derna

Later that year we decided an additional coaster would be very useful. Moss was contacted and I flew to England and together with John Armstrong, their main broker, went to Rotterdam to see a firm named Dammers & Van der Heide. John Dammers mentioned that friends of his owned a raised quarterdeck vessel barely a year old and named the *Elle*, registered in Helsinki. When efforts were made to re-register the vessel in Holland, the Finnish authorities refused the necessary export permit, so I decided to try my luck and left John Armstrong in the Atlanta Hotel, Rotterdam. It was the depth of winter and minus 23 degrees in Helsinki. My ears and large nose nearly froze off, and Finland was a completely new experience. I booked into the main hotel, which was also an experience. The bathroom was a little way down the corridor and obviously catered for more than one bedroom. When I wanted a bath, a large buxom Finnish woman would appear and conduct me a little way down the corridor and into a bathroom with steaming hot water in the bath, and a large wickerwork chair, over which a towel was draped. The Finnish woman then crossed her arms and waited and I eventually realised she was waiting for me to get into the bath. I was not used to this sort of thing but realised that there was no other way of having a bath, so I stepped into the bath. She then proceeded to scrub my back with a large brush, followed by similar treatment to my legs. On the command 'Aus' I was smothered in the large towel and given a rub over by my buxom attendant before regaining the privacy of the bedroom. After a day or two I became accustomed to the bath treatment and was no longer embarrassed.

I made daily visits to the ministry involved with the *Elle* and after three weeks they finally agreed and gave me an export permit. On my return to the Atlanta Hotel in Rotterdam I gave John a slap-up dinner. The dining room boasted a four-piece band and during dinner I asked for various tunes, such as 'A Room with a View', and success was only achieved by ordering a round of drinks for the band. Eventually we were the last to leave the dining room and I think John and I were 'very nicely thank you', and so were the band. The next morning as I came down to the foyer there was a sad bandmaster standing there saying they had all been given the sack. The manager was called and I explained to him that

I had just signed a contract for a new vessel and we had demanded the band play various tunes during dinner. The band was reinstated and, amusingly, when John and I appeared in the dining room that evening they struck up with 'A Room with a View' and all was forgiven. The *Elle* was purchased for £42,000 and renamed *Southern Isles*. We obtained a full cargo for Mombasa and I sailed with her and Captain Martin, a charming man who stayed with the company for many years, as far as Gibraltar where I left the ship and flew on to Kenya. The *Southern Isles* proved to be an outstanding vessel of 500 tons and was used mainly on voyages from Mombasa to Mahé in the Seychelles.

One day the managing director of Smith Mackenzie asked me if I would come to his office. I peddled down on my bicycle and was shown into a lofty office. He said, 'Young man, we greatly admire what you and your company have achieved but it has got to stop there. If you continue to try and take cargo away from the Conference Line we will have to break you.' I said, 'Thank you very much for asking me to come and I suggest you break me.'

The Southern Isles, *Mombasa*

The problem with coastal cargoes in those days was that the East African Conference Lines had a kind of monopoly, in that if a shipping agent shipped exclusively in a Conference Line vessel, at the end of six months they received a 10 per cent rebate on the freight rate. If, for example, they shipped once outside the Conference Lines then they lost their rebate.

As business expanded, we decided to purchase a third vessel in 1955 and through Moss I bought a French coaster that was having a complete engine refit in one of the old German submarine pens at St-Nazaire. She arrived in England from Guernsey with a cargo of potatoes, and after unloading these we loaded a cargo for East Africa and she was renamed *Southern Seas*.

In 1954 all petroleum products were carried in 45-gallon drums and the Conference freight rate was prohibitive. The Holland Africa Line had the monopoly of this by loading the drums into a lighter towed by a coaster. We decided this prohibitive freight rate could not continue and I approached Humphrey Byng, operations manager of Shell in Nairobi, and suggested that they should go into the coastal trade using a tanker that we would purchase. He explained that Shell's share of the trade did not warrant a tanker. We then suggested that if all the companies, Shell, Caltex and Standard-Vacuum Oil Co., pooled their requirements it would warrant building bulk depots in Tanga, Zanzibar, Pemba and Mtwara. The oil companies got together and came back agreeing to our proposal. Humphrey Byng pointed out that they could easily build the depots but we would have to provide the tanker moorings at each depot. We agreed, starting with Tanga.

We again contacted Moss in 1956, outlining the type of tanker we would require, and they came up with a vessel owned by the Anglo-Iranian Oil Company and laid up in Basra. It was German-built during the war, and had ten cargo tanks operated by pumps. This was Dick Bainbridge's territory and he went to Basra and duly bought the *Pazan*, which was renamed *Southern Pioneer*. The vessel was classified under Bureau Veritas for coastwise trading. She came down in ballast to Mombasa and was found by Lloyd's to be wrongly classified and only suitable for estuary trading and not coastal. This would involve

The Southern Pioneer

strengthening the ship, a costly undertaking. The Anglo-Iranian Oil Company was part of the Shell Group and I flew to London and met with Shell. I pointed out to them that the error was not of our making and I considered that whilst the wrong classification was not deliberate by Shell, they had sold the vessel to us classified for coastal trading. I pointed out that as a small company we could not afford to go to court with Shell and left it in their hands. Within a week Shell agreed to bear the cost of the work required to strengthen the ship for re-classification. The *Southern Pioneer* had several years running on the coast under a Greek master named Decol, with his son as engineer.

Bulk fuel depots were set up and we used the *Southern Pioneer* to lay the moorings in Tanga. The first shipment and all subsequent ones went very smoothly. Zanzibar came next and then Pemba, and eventually in 1959 we were asked by Shell to tender for bulk oil into the Red Sea ports of North Yemen, Mocha and Hodeidah. Besse, a French company who did virtually all the shipping out of Aden, was also asked to tender. We discovered that they had tendered more cheaply than we had by the use of Dracone Barges (floating flexible containers). Dick was doubtful if they would withstand the ultraviolet rays prevalent in the tropics. They were built in the Isle of Wight and we obtained a sample piece which we left on top of the wheelhouse of one of our coasters. Six months in the tropical sun caused it to break into small pieces. After six months of shipments by Besse using a dracone, it broke up off Mocha with a total spillage of oil, and we were given the contract.

The Yemenis can be difficult people to deal with and we found that after bulk tanks were installed in Hodeidah they could not always take the total quantity ordered, and so we decided the only way was to have a representative on the spot. Our agent in Hodeidah was Abdul Wasa, who was extremely pleasant, and we found that if we were absolutely straight with the Yemenis, they in the end trusted us. The best thing was to keep in contact with them and we made a habit of going up every six months to Sanaa to call on Ali, the government oil minister. I soon discovered that Ali, though a good Muslim, had a penchant for Dimple Haig and I always used to take him a couple of bottles in a brown paper bag, as of course alcohol is generally prohibited.

When we sold Southern Line to the East African Conference Lines in 1974, they insisted that we appoint Keith Trayner as the new chairman of the company. Keith had been employed by Southern Line for some time and he had originally worked for Union Castle. At the time of the sale I took Keith Trayner to Sanaa, with my two bottles of Haig, and called on Ali. I mentioned I had brought him his medicine. He thanked me very much and placed them in his drawer. I explained that Keith was the new head of the company but Ali did not seem at all interested. Six months later Keith went up on his own to see Ali, without any Haig. Ali said, 'Where's Buckle?' and Trayner replied that I was no longer with the company. 'Go away,' said Ali, 'send for Buckle.' When Keith got back to East Africa he contacted me and I flew to London and saw Sir Nicholas Kaiser to explain the situation. He said, 'That's all right, I will send Ted Lemon out to deal with the matter.' Ted Lemon was chairman of the Conference Lines, had worked his way up from a young clerk with Kaiser's, and to that day took perfect shorthand. Lemon arrived in Sanaa in his London suit and waistcoat and Ali took one look and refused to see him.

10

SOUTHERN LINE

By the early fifties we had a small shed near the Mombasa Yacht Club in which Dick had his engineering shop. As we needed more facilities, Dick heard about a garage with a corrugated iron roof next door to the Manor Hotel that was about to be demolished. We also found that an area known as the Tile Wharf, opposite African Marine in Mbaraki Creek, was no longer being used and obtained a long lease on the area. Dick bought the garage *in situ* and with some of our workers dismantled it and re-erected it on a heavy concrete floor, and we formed Southern Engineering Company Limited around 1954. There was a company in England which sold refurbished machinery and the workshop was fitted out with two large lathes and milling and welding machines. Another key man was John Chinaman, who was highly skilled on the lathes.

Dick approached a yacht club friend, Andy Crook, an ex-Royal Navy engineer who worked for African Marine, and asked whether he would join Southern Engineering. The deal was that he would be joint managing director with a low salary, but have a share of the profits. Andy jumped at the proposal and within three months had moved over and quickly suggested we make a side slip for vessels up to 100 feet utilising some old railway line obtained from railways and harbours.

One of the cargoes that readily came our way was bagged cement between Mombasa and Dar es Salaam. This was slow loading and invariably high-breakage but had very little value as cargo. Just north of Mombasa was the Bamburi Cement Company, a branch of the

Bamburi Cement Company

Portland Cement Co., whose chairman and managing director was Felix Mandl, an Austrian. Dick suggested the ideal way to ship cement was by bulk carrier. He had been in contact with a continental company who carried bulk cement – 3,000 tons of cement could be loaded in four and a half hours. I made a call to the cement company for an interview with Mandl and arranged to see him the following day.

Next day whilst in the waiting room before the meeting, I saw John Kalmanson, whom I had met some years previously, who made paper bags. He had sold his South African Company and he and his brother had started a new company called Canadian Overseas Packaging Industries. John visited both Mombasa and Nairobi, where he had branches. John said he had a meeting with Mandl following our own. Mandl was a cunning, elderly man, who we had been told had been incarcerated as a Jew by the Germans during the war and had some of his fingers broken. Our meeting went well and Mandl accepted my suggestion of a bulk carrier. We shook hands on the idea and were given the go-ahead.

When I left Mandl's office, John said, 'Was he in a good mood?' I said, 'Yes, I thought he was,' the irony being that John was trying to sell him paper bags for cement and we were trying to do away with them. Nevertheless John, to his credit, has remained a close friend ever since.

In 1960 Dick flew to Hamburg and inspected a large cargo ship. Southern Line bought the vessel, of the raised quarterdeck type, for conversion to a bulk cement carrier. This involved a cofferdam being built amidships which would separate the forward and after hold in which two pumps would be installed. The two holds would be altered by installing thick canvas angled at 5 degrees towards the centre cofferdam, supported on steel frames with the bottom of each hold angled down to the cofferdam. The bulk cement would be poured into the holds and prior to discharge would be aerated with low-pressure air through the canvas. This enabled the bottom part of the bulk cement in each hold to flow like water down to a screw pump that pumped the cement into large pipes at high air pressure. Cement would be blown through the top of the storage silo and the whole discharge would take about nine hours. There was no claim for loss or breakage and the quick handling enabled us to run at a reasonable profit. The ship was named *Southern Baobab* and carried 2,200 tons of bulk cement. One morning Felix Mandl telephoned the office and complained about the slow rate of discharge into their silo at Dar es Salaam. Dick went aboard during the next discharge and raised the pressure in the air pumps. This resulted in the top of the cement silo being blown off, as there had been a slight blockage in one of their pipes.

Cessna 170, Mombasa

In 1958 I took up flying again and regained my Private Pilot's Licence in Nairobi. My first long overseas trip was in 1960 to Naples for the Olympics in a single-engine Cessna 170, registered 5Y-KNK, with a tail wheel. I was representing East Africa, sailing in the Flying

Dutchman class. I had been pestered by a girlfriend, Betty Brierley, in Nairobi to take her along, and reluctantly agreed. We set off from Wilson airport in Nairobi with the first stop at Juba and a night stop at a government rest house at Malakal on the Nile, with the windows wired against mosquitoes. It was extremely hot and humid. I went into dinner on my own and on sitting down was joined by a large and extremely dark African, who proved excellent company.

I found out he was the Chief Justice from Khartoum sent down to investigate some cattle theft money. He kept calling me 'Sir.' In the end I said, 'Why do you call me sir? You are the Chief Justice and I am just an ordinary person.' He said, 'Sir, when you British left, you left three wonderful things that we admire to this day: a sense of justice, a sense of fair play, and a sense of humour. That is why I call you sir.'

Our next landing was near Khartoum to refuel and then to Luxor, where we stopped for a day and stayed at the Winter Palace Hotel, a large and empty hotel as it was the hottest time of the year. We spent a celibate night in two large double beds under mosquito nets and next morning visited the Valley of the Kings. This meant crossing the river by a sailing felucca, and then by a rattly old open American car along a track, known as a road, to the Valley of the Kings. I cannot remember the first two tombs we went to see, except at the entrance there was an Egyptian in his robes with a pressure lamp that he pumped up and lit, and as we walked into the tomb it became cooler. By holding up the lamp, we could see beautiful paintings on the sides of the walls and ceilings. We visited a couple more tombs, after which I felt extremely unwell and to my embarrassment deposited my breakfast on the ground. We returned to the hotel in the rattling taxi and I opted for bed. Luckily Betty managed to acquire another room and left me to my fate. I realised that dinner was obviously the cause of my complaint and I had an unsettled stomach for the rest of the evening.

The next morning, feeling better, we set off for Tobruk where we refuelled and obtained four 4-gallon demijohns of fuel that were stowed behind our seats. As we had a long trip ahead of us I obtained permission to take off along the taxiway and to fly over the Gulf of Sirte to Marble Arch, a wartime disused airstrip. On arrival we flew low over

Tony Bentley-Buckle, Naples Olympics 1960

the various runways and picked the one with the least potholes. We landed and refuelled from the demijohns using a funnel and a chamois leather as a filter. The various buildings were in a dilapidated state with the occasional steel helmet lying on the ground. On looking inland one could see the elaborate Marble Arch built by the Italians during the Second World War which, I think, marked the boundary with Libya. This was subsequently destroyed by Gaddafi after he seized power in 1969. We arrived in Naples where Betty and I parted and arranged to meet in Malta at the end of the Olympics. I immediately refuelled the aircraft, which is a must, because if the tanks are left half-empty condensation can form.

After the Olympics, in which I came 15th out of 32, and having sold my Kenya boat, I flight-planned to Malta and took off down the coast of Italy. After about half-an-hour's flight the fuel tank gauge seemed far lower than I expected and I realised that some fuel had been stolen while the plane was hangared in Naples. The only thing for me to do was to put down in Sicily. I found an airstrip that appeared to be out of use and took a taxi to a filling station where I purchased two demijohns of petrol and refuelled the aircraft. I considered this rather yellowish-looking petrol would mix with what was left in my tanks to give me sufficient to get to Malta. Happily, this was the case and when I landed in Malta the tanks showed a quarter full. After refuelling I gave a sigh of relief and went in search of Betty. On the leg down the Nile, Betty became irritating and I looked forward to arriving back in Nairobi. However, we had a night stop at Juba where a couple ran a mission. Before supper that evening we knelt down and listened to a fairly long talk to God. The next morning the aircraft refused to start and we had to summon help from our host of the evening before.

He first insisted that we all kneel down and started, 'Dear God, you know I am not much of an engineer but I will try my best and I pray that my best will be good enough to get Tony back to Nairobi.' He dismantled the engine and found one of the valves sticking. After what seemed a long time he put everything together again and then insisted that we kneel down again. I was becoming a little brassed off by this time but had to endure another monologue to God. He said, 'Dear God, I hope I have done enough and Tony and his friend arrive back safely. There is nothing more that I can say.'

Lo and behold, the wretched thing started and we took off. Betty began niggling again, and once airborne I am afraid I said, 'Betty, I hope we don't meet again.' She was rather upset at this but stopped from then on. When we arrived in Nairobi, I refuelled, said goodbye, and took off for Mombasa.

On 2 November 1960 Godfrey Place arrived in Mombasa aboard the aircraft carrier HMS *Albion*. We had been in Marlag prison camp together and he had been awarded the Victoria Cross for his part in the attack on the German battleship *Tirpitz* by X-craft, midget submarines, in Kaa Fiord, Norway in September 1943. I took him up with another friend in the Cessna for a local trip and on the return Godfrey said to me, 'Tony, do you think you could land on the carrier?' I told him no problem, even though it was at anchor in Kilindini, and we did a fly past before landing. However, we had a small problem: I couldn't take off without a headwind. Godfrey said the plane could be stowed below and the following morning when the ship was at sea I could fly off. I took a boat out to the ship to find the aircraft on the flight deck. We proceeded out of the harbour and after a farewell chat with Godfrey, I climbed in and as we turned into wind, started up and took off. I circled the ship, gave a final wave and landed back at Port Reitz airport near Mombasa.

In May 1961 Frank Champion, number two in Smith Mackenzie, and his wife Esme asked me to dinner one evening and on arrival Esme introduced me to Lady Margaret Stamer, who had just arrived from Nairobi. We spent most of the evening talking and within a few days I decided Margaret was the girl for me. We were married just over five weeks later on 30 June 1961 – it would have been earlier had I not forgotten to put up the wedding bans in the District Commissioner's office. It would have looked very odd if I had obtained a special licence! For our honeymoon we decided to fly to Inanzoro, Paradise Island, in Portuguese East Africa. We stayed the first night in the Zanzibar Club and realised we had left all the necessary flight charts behind.

Tony and Margaret Bentley-Buckle's wedding, Mombasa, 30 June 1961
(Dick Bainbridge, Tony, Margaret and Pat, Tony's sister)

Tony and Margaret Bentley-Buckle, Beaulieu, July 2007

Our friend Basil Bell, with whom we had had dinner the night before, kindly provided us with a Shell road map. The next day we took off for Lumbo in Mozambique, where we stayed at the only hotel, an old farmhouse. A huge netted terrace was occupied by masses of birds that nested in the surrounding pot plants. They perched on the chairs and tables and helped themselves to any titbits. The next day as we flew down the Mozambique Channel the weather deteriorated, the start of a cyclone, and we decided to divert to Salisbury with the help of the road map. We stayed at Meikles Hotel, where we were given the honeymoon suite. Margaret had been in Southern Rhodesia before, and her grandmother had a farm nearby, as did a good friend called Bill Kensington.

The four of us had lunch together, tucking in to oysters. When they were finished I said to grandmamma, 'Would you like another dozen?' She put her lorgnettes to her eyes and said, 'Tell me, young man, are you stinking rich?'

Margaret, Deborah, Tony and Nicholas Bentley-Buckle, Mombasa, 1963

I said that I had enough to give us what we wanted. We stayed with good friends of Margaret, Ruth and Nick O'Connor, and rescued Margaret's VW Beetle, which was in a packing case on their farm. Armed with the correct charts, we returned to Mombasa.

Nicholas our son was born on 21 March 1962 at the Katherine Bibby Hospital in Mombasa, as was our daughter Deborah on 25 March the following year. Nick went to school at St Andrew's, Turi, north-west of Nairobi, and in due course Deborah followed. In 1970 Nick went to the Downs School, Bristol and then followed in my footsteps to Ampleforth in 1976. Deborah went to a prep school at Burnham-on-Sea, followed by Rosemead School near Littlehampton. After leaving Ampleforth, Nick joined the Royal Green Jackets infantry regiment in Winchester and later worked as an insurance broker with Lloyd's of London, eventually becoming a yacht broker in Southampton. After leaving school Deborah attended secretarial college in London and later emigrated to South Africa, where she still lives.

I considered Southern Line needed a larger plane and in October 1961 heard that a farmer known as Mongoose Snowdon, at Nanyuki in the Rift Valley, had for sale a Cessna 210, 5Y-APG, a single-engine aeroplane, with a retractable undercarriage. One snag we discovered was that bumpy airstrips could cause trouble when retracting the main undercarriage. Snowdon was due in court in Nairobi for an incident at Nanyuki. It appeared that Reggie Smart, a retired air vice-marshal on a nearby farm, heard firing one night and went to Snowdon's house, then telephoned the Nanyuki telephone exchange. No answer. They took their revolvers, went down to the telephone exchange and on looking through the window found the African operator fast asleep over his switchboard. Mongoose fired a shot into the room, whereupon the telephone operator took off through the opposite window without opening it and of course accused the white man of trying to shoot him. He was duly summonsed and I met him at the Muthaiga Country Club in Nairobi the night before his case, and we had a drink together. He said the great thing at Nanyuki now was if you rang the telephone exchange at any time, there was an immediate response of 'Number please?' I gather he got off with a caution.

Papa Golf was an excellent fast aeroplane and I flew to Aden a couple of times on various trips and to Kismayo in Somaliland, where Southern Line had an Italian agent. On one trip a Somali woman was in the airport building and round her neck was a pretty necklace of golden balls. As gold was reasonably cheap in those days in Somalia, I remarked to our agent that I would like to buy something similar for Margaret. After a little jabbering in Somali the necklace was removed, handed to me and the agent said, '300 shillings'. This I willingly handed over and Margaret has the necklace to this day – however, she did have to scrub it well and re-string it.

Towards the end of March 1964, Gerry Read of Shell Oil, Nairobi, rang me and said they were looking at the possibility of putting bulk fuel into Perim Island from Aden and asked me what I thought. I suggested we fly up and have a look. Perim had been a major coaling port for nearly eighty years, supplying Welsh coal in the days of steam ships, and it had also been a base for a large salvage company that had operated out of Mombasa in times past. On 1 April Margaret and I flew to Nairobi and on to Lake Rudolf, where we night-stopped at the fishing camp. The following day we flew on to Addis Ababa and that afternoon into Aden. Two days later I flew the Shell representatives to Perim to look at the site, and see if one of our small tankers could get into the port. I said this would be no trouble, and before we left for Aden we wandered round the island and found a disused racecourse and evidence of what had been a thriving community.

On arriving back in Aden we had drinks with the Shell manager, and Margaret, having previously obtained signed copies of the artist David Shepherd's prints of Mukalla and Shibaam,[46] was keen to fly into the Hadramaut.[47] I was not too happy at the idea, as we would have to obtain permission from the local agent at Mukalla up the coast. One of the Shell wives said she would love to join us, so we left early the next morning.

On the trip up the coast the weather became worse and blew a gale, and on looking inland up the wadis, normally dry at this time of year, a torrent of water could be seen coming down. By this time I needed to land at the RAF station at Riyan for fuel, as I would have insufficient for the return to Aden or into the Hadramaut for that matter. As we circled over the airfield, there was nobody to be seen and the runway of sand and mud was glistening ominously. We had no alternative but to try and land, and after another circuit, the place erupted with people running everywhere, first aid vans came out, and it was obvious that the airfield had been closed. I said to the girls that there was only one way we could land and that was across the runway and on to a hard parking area, otherwise we could nose over in the soft ground with dire consequences. This we did and it worked perfectly with Papa Golf slowing in the muddy runway with sufficient time on the hard standing of the parking area to bring the aircraft to a halt.

A very irate-looking flight lieutenant came striding out and as I opened my little window he said, 'Can't you see that the airport is closed?' He then saw the two girls and said, 'There is a dance tonight.' The closure of the airport had been put out by radio, but we were too far from Aden to pick up any weather report. They welcomed us into the mess and we had a marvellous lunch of crayfish.

Nobby Clark, the flight lieutenant in charge, who later became a good friend and visited us in Mombasa, said that they often showed films in the evening to which they invited the Bedouin Arabs. On one occasion during the showing of a Wild West film there was the sound of rifle fire and after the show they found the screen was riddled with bullet holes as the Bedouin had been firing at the outlaws. From then on whenever the Bedouin attended a film, they were asked to leave their rifles outside, guarded by one of them, in case of a repetition. After lunch the following day the weather had improved sufficiently for us to refuel and fly back to Aden, as the weather in the hills of the Hadramaut was still too bad to allow us in.

11

SOUTHERN LINE II

Having my pilot's licence helped immensely with our idea of starting the East Africa National Shipping Line and in our small aeroplane I clocked up seventy-two visits between Nairobi, Dar es Salaam, Kampala and Zambia. The East African Conference Lines based in Kaiser House, London decided that Southern Line should be admitted as a member and thereafter our main coastwise problem no longer existed. We started to flex our muscles a little and decided to go into the ocean trade between East Africa and Europe involving 15,000–20,000 ton vessels. We believed there was no way we could get into the European Conference trade without the four East African governments being involved. George Kahama, Minister of Transport in Tanzania, liaised on behalf of the governments involved. Our offer was to give each government a 10 per cent shareholding, with Southern Line having the remaining 60 per cent, and a seven-year management contract of the proposed company.

Somehow Conference Lines heard of our negotiations and the chairman, John Bevan, made several visits to East Africa in order to find out what was going on. In London I had formed the Inter-Governmental Standing Committee on Shipping, called ISCOS for short. John Bevan finally arrived in Dar es Salaam in the hope of persuading the governments to make a decision. I suggested to him that we jointly meet George Kahama in Dar es Salaam. After biting our nails until six in the evening, we saw George emerge to announce that the four governments had accepted the Southern Line proposal.

I considered the Conference Lines must in some way be involved to stop cut-throat competition, which would do no one any good. It was finally agreed that each Conference Line would in turn vacate a berth to enable the National Line to take it up. This envisaged voyages between East Africa and Europe. For example, if Union Castle vacated its berth on one voyage, a National Line vessel would use the Union Castle agent in London as the agent for that voyage. The next thing was to find a vessel. I went to London and discussed the position with H. E. Moss. We required a vessel that would carry 500,000 tons bale space, which equated to around 12,500 dead-weight tons. We also thought it should carry twelve passengers, the reason being that with no more than twelve passengers there was no need for a doctor on board. We knew many of the companies offered a free trip to their agent, to keep them happy.

The East African National Shipping Line ship, Harambee, *arriving at Mombasa*

We bought the 10,000-ton German-built vessel *Santa Barbara*, to be registered in Kenya as the *Harambee*. She arrived in 1967 on her maiden voyage to Mombasa and a presidential reception was held on board with Jomo Kenyatta presiding. Gradually Southern Line was becoming more important each year. The local chairman of the East African Conference Lines was the ex-local director of the Union Castle Line, Trevor Dejean. He had married Biddy, the ex-matron of Mombasa Hospital. Every year Sir Nicholas Kaiser, chairman of the Union Castle Line, paid a visit to Mombasa and gave a dinner party for Trevor. I was invited and frequently had a slight difference of opinion with Kaiser. Afterwards I was reprimanded by Biddy, saying, 'You never argue with Sir Nicholas.' After they were transferred to South Africa I was appointed the new chairman of the Line. Biddy, on hearing this, said, 'How can somebody like you be appointed to replace my Trevor?' Shortly after their arrival in South Africa, Trevor died of a heart attack. In April 1964 Margaret and I decided to fly to England in Papa Golf for the summer and we invited two great friends, John and Lydia Ward. We set off on 16 May with John in the co-pilot's seat and the girls behind. We had a trouble-free journey along the Nile and decided to spend a weekend on the island of Corfu. After landing I decided that after the long desert trip it would be prudent to change the oil, which I did, assisted by two Shell men, whilst John and the girls sat in a café under a large mulberry tree. Before I finished a man arrived in his car and introduced himself as John Damaskinos, the director of tourism for the island. He was charming and spoke excellent English. We said we wanted to stay in a little village near the casino down the coast and he insisted on driving us there. Having settled in, the girls decided they would go for a swim from a small jetty below the hotel. Being used to warm tropical waters, they dived in and there were shrieks and they nearly walked on the water, it was so cold!

Next day John, our host, arrived and told us of a nice little place, the Avra Hotel run by the Spinoula brothers at Benitses, down the coast. We booked in and found it completely unspoilt and we ate outside on a vine-covered patio. The Greek food was washed down with plenty of wine, and we took a great liking to the two brothers. Our first requirement was transport, and the four of us took a taxi into Corfu and hired two Vespa scooters. Lydia sat behind John and Margaret sat side-saddle behind me and for a time kept adjusting her position which caused me to wobble around on the road. Margaret, who has always loved various shrubs and plants, had a habit of saying

'Stop!' and on skidding to a halt would nip across the road to the garden of some private house and break off a cutting. To this day we have a bush grown from one of our Corfu cuttings.

During dinner at the hotel there was a lot of chit-chat going on in the kitchen and we asked one of the brothers what the problem was. He said their sister, who ran the kitchen, had heard their mother was very ill on the Greek mainland, and could not get over until the next weekly Dakota arrived, and would then have to go via Athens. We told the brothers that she should pack her suitcase and be ready to leave early the following morning when I would fly her over to the nearest airstrip in Greece and leave her there. One of the brothers drove us to the airport and said he would remain until we returned. The poor sister seemed a little frightened at the size of the aircraft in which she was going to fly but nevertheless climbed in and we took off. My passenger pointed out where the nearest airstrip was and we landed. With profuse Corfu thanks and a slapping kiss she departed from the airstrip carrying her suitcase, and without any flight plan I took off and nipped back to Corfu, where the brother was waiting for me. He asked me how much it would cost for the flight and I said, 'Don't be silly, we did it just to help you.' They never forgot this gesture and on all our subsequent flights to Corfu we always stayed at the Avra, and to our embarrassment the brothers always insisted that the first evening with wine was on them and no payment was necessary.

The usual routine after dinner was for the family and Nico the waiter to do Greek dancing, waving their white handkerchiefs in between glasses of retsina. One evening we all decided to go to the casino, which had been a luxury royal villa where Prince Philip had been born. Margaret bet using her time of birth, 3.30 in the morning, and won a small amount. Thereafter whenever we arrived in Corfu we would fly low past the hotel, waggling our wings from side to side to announce our arrival. On one occasion when we arrived in a hire car, Nico, carrying an armful of plates, was the first to see us. These he dropped on the ground with a crash in true Greek fashion and gave Margaret a great smacking kiss. As we prepared to leave for the onward flight to England via Italy and Geneva, we were held up by Prince

Constantine and his wife who obviously had right of way, and kept us waiting at least twenty-five minutes.

On arrival in Geneva we stayed at the Hotel des Bergues overlooking the lake. Looking out from our bedroom we could see the large lake fountain that came on every morning. The service at the hotel was excellent and when on our subsequent trip we again booked into the hotel and presented our passports, the receptionist waved them away and said 'We have all your particulars.' After two days in Geneva we set off for Lympne. We had to climb over the Alps at 14,000 feet and the obvious lack of oxygen showed when Margaret and Lydia played a game of draughts behind us. One would hear, 'I huff you', a pause, and the other would say, 'Oh yes, and I huff you.' It was obviously useless to play draughts at that height without oxygen. However, all went well and we arrived at Lympne.

We met up for the return trip three weeks later and stopped in Cairo, where we tried to climb the pyramids. Margaret had done this as a small girl aged eight, but none of us got very far up as each block was at least waist high, and we ran out of energy less than halfway up and Lydia suffered from vertigo. We also visited the fascinating Valley of the Kings at Luxor before continuing south.

The colour scheme of our aircraft was dark brown on top of the wings and when the tanks were opened for inspection the wings were so hot that they could barely be touched. We cleared for Wadi Halfa in the Sudan and as I started the climb the engine kept spitting and I realised the fuel was so hot it was vaporising. Luckily as we gained height everything cooled down and the engine smoothed out. A lesson learnt: do not leave a hot wing in the tropical sun before take-off. We flew past Abu Simbel and had been told in Cairo there was a UN programme to remove the temple and huge statues to higher ground, as where they were situated was shortly to be flooded by the new Aswan dam. As we flew past we realised that it would be the last time we saw them in their original position. After we landed at Wadi Halfa the control tower informed us that there was a haboob (dust storm) over Sudan and we would have to wait until it cleared. After a long wait Air Traffic Control advised that it was safe to continue on to Khartoum.

Abu Simbel

Margaret & 5Y-AEV

However, I soon discovered that even flying at 12,000 feet the dust was so thick that I could hardly see the wing tips. The navigation from Abu Simbel to Khartoum was by means of radio beacons. Arriving over Khartoum, I let down in slow circles until it was clear enough to see the airport. We taxied off the main runway and I decided to clean the air filter. After removing it and rinsing it in a bucket of petrol an alarming amount of sand was found in the bottom. Happily, we had no further problems and arrived back in Mombasa on 15 June.

In November that year Margaret decided to learn to fly and acquired her Private Pilot's Licence with top marks for engines and airframes. Thereafter she did all the navigation when we flew together. Although Papa Golf was an excellent aircraft, Margaret felt it was wrong for us to fly around the world in a single-engine aircraft leaving two young children at home. I agreed and as the chairman of Southern Line, persuaded the board that we should purchase a twin-engined aircraft. There was a new twin-engined Piper Comanche, 5Y-AEV, available with wing-tip tanks that had a seven-hour safe range. The Piper agent, Caryl Waterpark, checked me out to amend my licence to a twin rating. To my mind it is only really safe to fly if one's reactions are immediate. My examiner would carry on with small-talk such as, 'Whose farm do you think is that down there?' Whilst I was looking down he would cut the fuel on one engine and I had to react fast and check all the switches to find out what had gone amiss.

In 1965 Noel Coward arrived in Mombasa with a friend of ours and came to lunch. On leaving he told us he had enjoyed himself so much and asked if he could come again. He expressed an interest in seeing wildlife and we flew him up to Tsavo National Park. David Sheldrick, the park warden, arranged to have some tame

Noel Coward

baby elephants and rhino at the strip as we landed. Noel was ecstatic as he tickled and patted their noses.[48] We then saw a toucan, which Coward called the La Di Dah bird. We kept in touch and on a trip to London we were invited to dinner with him. Unfortunately he had to cancel as the Queen Mother had asked him to join her. We thought it was just an excuse until we saw their picture in the papers next day.

In 1967 we flew to England with Margaret navigating via, of course, Corfu. I had no instrument rating for flying in bad weather over Europe but felt happy enough to fly as if I had one. We had now abandoned using small airstrips like Lympne and flight-planned to Gatwick.

I remember on one occasion I had bought a large demijohn of ouzo in Corfu and I reported to customs that I would be staying for twelve days. On being asked if there was anything to declare I caused much head-scratching when I said, 'A demijohn of ouzo.'

I told customs that the aircraft would be locked and rather than put my demijohn in customs I would give them a key to the aircraft. They said, 'That's all right, we trust you.'

That year we ordered a new Daimler Sovereign costing £1,200 from Jaguar to be delivered to Gatwick on our arrival. We took delivery of the car and used it during our stay in England, after which it was shipped to Kenya. While we were in England the Arab–Israeli Six Day War broke out and all flying was prohibited over the North African coast.[49] This meant flying via Madrid and Gibraltar and across to Las Palmas for fuel, before flying to Dakar and on to Douala and Yaoundé in Cameroon. The flight to Gibraltar was forbidden at Madrid, thanks to Britain's long-term occupation of the Rock, and I was locked up for two hours for filing a flight plan to Gibraltar.

A kindly gent suggested flight-planning to North Africa and then calling Gibraltar over the Mediterranean and asking for clearance to land. This we did, before going on Las Palmas. The flight to Douala past Accra in Ghana meant that aircraft in transit had to take a dogleg course over the sea fifteen miles offshore. The weather was very poor and as there was thick cloud I decided to cut the corner and fly in a straight line past Accra. Stupidly I called them estimating abeam, only to be told that I must land or else they would scramble jets to force us to do so. Luckily in the bad weather there was a British Airways flight due in shortly, and following a second insistent call to land I increased speed and called back, 'Accra, Accra reading you strength 2, repeat again, Accra, Accra reading you strength 2.'

By this time I was slightly past Accra and called back, 'Accra, Accra, cannot read you. Turn to frequency 1181', which I knew they had not got. By this time they were so busy with the British Airways flight that we were soon safely out of range, with Margaret saying, 'It was your own damn fault, you should have kept off the coast.'

That morning, 3 July, we had decided to take off early from Abidjan, and when we came down to reception from our hotel room to pay the bill I asked for a taxi to the airport. We were descended on by several taxi drivers, the first saying, 'Moi, Monsieur, mille cinq cent francs.' Another cut in and said, 'Moi, Monsieur, mille quatre cent francs.' By this time Margaret was hopping up and down as one piece of luggage went towards one taxi and another piece to another taxi. I am afraid I rather enjoyed the Dutch auction and when one said, 'Moi, Monsieur, neuf cent francs', I said, 'You are my boy', and we miraculously collected our luggage and all the way to the airport Margaret told me how stupid I was and that we might have lost all our luggage.

After this epic day we night-stopped at Yaoundé, a small airport virtually in the jungle. In the baggage lounge, which was also the waiting room, there was a well-dressed African and a rather tatty African baggage clerk to whom I said I wanted a taxi into town. The well-dressed African snapped his fingers and instructed the baggage handler to take out our cases. Margaret said, 'Now stop it, find out how much it is and do not let them touch our luggage until you have sorted it out.' By this time our baggage was disappearing out the entrance to the airport building followed by the well-dressed African. When we followed them out there was a large glistening Mercedes car with a flag on it and the well-dressed African said, 'My driver will take you into town.' I apologised profusely for the rude way I had acted, and when we got into his car I asked the driver who his boss was. He replied, 'The Minister of Justice', and I said to Margaret, 'You can't win.' We spent a basic night in a hotel at Yaoundé and took off again early the next morning, eastward across Cameroon towards Entebbe. The weather had changed and was very sunny.

Margaret and I were thankful that we were in a twin-engined aircraft as we flew mile after mile over African jungle. Had we been in a single-engine aircraft and needed to land near an African village, we would still be there to this day. After refuelling at Entebbe we went on to Mombasa. One thing we had to be careful of was flying over Lake Victoria from Entebbe, where swarms of lake flies were to be avoided at all costs as they could cause engine failure. Having previously flown into a swarm in our single-engine Papa Golf I had to go round in a very wide circle looking for rain clouds in order to clean the windscreen.

In September 1967 Southern Line was asked to quote for the removal of 200 tons of fuel oil from a stranded Liberty ship, the *Costoula*, at Malindi. The ship was one of a class built by the hundred in the United States during the Second World War and was in very poor condition. Having inspected the ship, we signed a Lloyd's salvage agreement to refloat the vessel. Andy Crook and Keith Trayner and I boarded the ship for a preliminary survey. The inspection showed the engine room and shaft tunnel partially flooded and with insufficient fresh water on board to fire up the boiler. It was decided to lay a steel pipe across the seabed and supply the ship with 200 tons of fresh water from the *Southern Pioneer*. The ship's anchors were laid out ahead and a portable diesel pump connected to the ship's pipes and water discharged. The forepeak was filled to trim the ship by the head and a boiler lit and steam supplied to the windlass. On 6 October *Costoula* began to move as both anchors were hauled in and by late afternoon the vessel was afloat. The *Southern Baobab* towed the ship to Mombasa where it was anchored in Port Reitz. Legal proceedings took eighteen months to resolve before the vessel was eventually sold and towed to Hong Kong for scrap.

That same year we were interested in purchasing a further vessel of 550,000 bale for the East Africa National Shipping Line and H. E. Moss came up with the sister-ship to the *Harambee*, which was due in Durban in a couple of days' time. I decided to inspect her and prepared to leave the following day from Mombasa. This would involve a flight to Virginia airport in Durban. John Ward, who was then our company doctor, heard we were going and asked if we had a spare seat. I told him he was welcome to come with us and John, Margaret and I took off the following day, which happened to be a Saturday. We flew straight down to Blantyre where we refuelled and flight-planned for Virginia airport in Durban. As we approached the South African boundary we came under a new Flight Information Region boundary controlled from Salisbury, and duly reported to Salisbury.

A few minutes later Margaret said, 'What are we doing this evening?' I replied, 'It's a weekend and we are booked into the Edward Hotel in Durban.'[50] She said, 'Why don't we go into Lourenço Marques for the evening and have prawns piri piri?'[51] I said that we would have to divert, which meant overtime for Lourenço Marques for customs and immigration, a taxi into town and the cost of a hotel for the night. Margaret turned to John in the back seat and said, 'John, would you like prawns piri piri?' John said, 'Oh yes.' I contacted Salisbury and said, 'Five Yankee Alpha Echo Victor, flight-planned Blantyre, Durban, wish to divert to Lourenço Marques.' Salisbury replied, 'Echo Victor, reason for diversion?' I replied, 'My wife wants prawns piri piri.' The Salisbury controller replied, 'Echo Victor permission granted, you poor sucker.'

I then called Lourenço Marques giving our ETA and said we would be night-stopping. When we landed I had to sign and pay for overtime for the customs and immigration, landing fees, and the inevitable taxi into town. I believe we stayed at the Polana Hotel and went out for prawns piri piri.[52] I must say these were delicious and I was forced, against my better judgement, to agree with Margaret and John. I telephoned the Edward Hotel informing them we would be arriving the next day due to bad weather. On the Sunday morning, with more overtime payments to immigration, we took off for the short flight to Virginia airport. We arrived at the Edward Hotel a day late to be told that it was perfectly all right as they had kept the room for us the previous evening. This made our prawns piri piri bill hardly worthwhile.

I contacted Guy Radmore of John T. Rennie & Co., who informed us the vessel was due in that evening and were arranging for us to inspect her the following day.[53] When I told Margaret she said, 'There you are, there was no need for us to have been here earlier and if you had organised things better we could have flight-planned for Lourenço Marques without all the hoo-ha and trouble!' This saga came to a happy conclusion when I inspected the ship the following day. Being Danish-owned, she was in excellent condition and we agreed with London that we would negotiate through H. E. Moss and purchase her. We spent a couple more days in Durban and picked up John Ward, who told us that he and Lydia had arranged to join a South African medical practice after he had sorted out his affairs in Kenya. We returned via Salisbury and Lilongwe. In March 1968 the new ship was commissioned as the *Uganda* by President Obote at Dar es Salaam. The international newspapers were present and Margaret's leg made the press with an unusual picture while waiting for the president. The following year we added to the National Line with another Danish-built vessel, *Minnesota*, which became the *Mulungushi* for Zambia, and in 1970 we purchased the *Ujamaa* for Tanzania.

Margaret's legs

Our cargo vessels had been trading well around the Indian Ocean and the Red Sea and in 1967 we ordered our first new-build vessel, a tanker from the German yard of Kröger-Werft on the Kiel Canal. On the afternoon of 12 December 1968, the canal traffic was stopped for three minutes while Margaret christened the ship *Southern Cross* and she slipped down the ways. Two weeks later she was taken on sea trials by Keith Trayner and duly sailed for East Africa.

Launching of the Southern Cross, *German yard of Kröger-Werft on the Kiel Canal, 12 December 1968*

12

AN ITALIAN AFFAIR

I had, from time to time, been receiving brochures from Alistair Easton about various yachts on his books and he had one named *Tresca*, meaning an illicit affair in Italian. She was built in 1937 by J. Miller & Sons at St Monans in Fife, Scotland, for Dr T. H. Ward, of Weston House, near Totnes, Devon. Her port of registry was Dartmouth, but in 1938 was changed to Brixham with Ward still the owner. She was a 73-foot Bermudan cutter with a 92-foot mast and a sail area of 2,500 square feet, and laid up in Malta.

In June 1968, as the time was drawing near for our usual holiday jaunt to Europe, we planned to fly via Malta. On arriving in Cairo we refuelled and flight-planned direct to Malta. Halfway across the Mediterranean between Cairo and Malta, air traffic asked us to confirm that our destination was Malta. On confirming affirmative they came back and said due to bad weather Malta was closed and asked us for our alternative. I replied Sicily, and they again came back saying that Sicily was closed due to low cloud and again asked for another alternative. I asked Margaret to refer to our airfield guide and the nearest place to land was the American base at Wheelus Field near Tripoli. I immediately altered course and calculated the distance, and it became clear our fuel would not give us a reserve, so we had no alternative but to get to Tripoli. I leaned out the mixture as much as I dared and switched over to the tip tanks.

We continued on these and flew with one wing slightly down to drain the tank to zero. When that tank started to cough I quickly

Tresca

switched to the opposite tip tank and flew with that wing low until the engine started to cough then I switched back to the main. International Air Radio asked for our latest estimate of fuel remaining and we told them it would be marginal and they said that they would alert the rescue helicopter in case we had to ditch. Having exhausted the auxiliary tanks, we were left with what remained in the main tanks. I kept flying one wing low, then the other wing low, anticipating that we would get into the position where one of the engines started coughing and we would be left with the one remaining tank for our arrival. We advised the tower when Tripoli came in sight and we landed on the nearest runway, having been given priority. Margaret and I were a little anxious and I have to confess that my mouth was very dry. I opened the inspection covers of the wing tanks and found one tank completely dry and the engine must have been about to stop, while the other tank had less than an eighth of an inch of fuel remaining.

International Air Radio, which ran the airport, offered us a lift into town for the night. They were most helpful and took us to one of the best hotels and told us their controller's transport would pick us up early next morning and return us to the airport. We ordered a snack and some wine in our room, and the transport arrived at 7.30 the next morning. Our problems were not yet over, for as we checked out at customs and immigration we were asked why we had no visas. The Arab staff put all sorts of difficulties in our way. Margaret turned to the immigration officer saying, 'It is no wonder you do not get many tourists here, you are worse than the gippoes.' Luckily he did not understand what Margaret was saying and we were given clearance, having filed a flight plan for Malta. I contacted International Air Radio, thanked them for their help and requested permission to taxi for take-off. There was no cloud forecast over Malta and they gave us clearance and wished us a good trip.

Two years later Margaret flew us into Dar es Salaam in a small single-engine aircraft. On our departure Margaret called the tower and a controller asked for our names. She said, 'Bentley-Buckle.' The tower replied, 'Roger, we last met in Tripoli when I was working there. The next time you come down let us know and we will have a meal together.'

When we eventually arrived in Malta I got in touch with the broker and arranged to inspect the yacht. Margaret came with me and it was love at first sight. She was laid up in one of the creeks, with her mast lying on deck overhanging the bow and the stern, and the hull was copper sheathed. I realised there was very little work needed apart from scarfing in a piece of silver spruce in the mast. I also learnt that one of our National Line ships on the European service was due to call in at Malta to pick up a new harbour tug for the Kenya Railways and Harbours. When we left I arranged to come back at the same time as the National Line vessel called for the tug. The ship had a 50-ton heavy lift derrick and was under the command of Captain Martin, an ex-Southern Line master. *Tresca* was towed round to the ship's berth.

As we watched, a bystander said to me, 'There goes a beautiful sea boat.' I said, 'How do you know?' He said, 'I did a trip across the Atlantic in her once.'

In a way this reassured Margaret as she does not particularly like the sea, especially in heavy weather. Stevedores throughout the world can whack up the charges for any heavy lift, but Captain Martin assured me that he would not require stevedores for lifting *Tresca* as his crew operated the heavy lift derrick. The captain decided that it would be necessary to cut out a section of the ship's rail and weld in a cradle to hold *Tresca* safely, with heavy wires from the mast to the yacht to hold her securely. Having loaded the tug, the stevedore foreman went over and put his hand on *Tresca* and said, 'Now we have touched your yacht we will put in a bill for handling her.'

I said nothing. The crew lifted *Tresca*, secured her and sailed for Mombasa. The captain told me that he personally would check *Tresca* about three times a day as he was terrified of his position should anything happen to her. Needless to say, after the ship sailed I told the agent that should the stevedores put in charges for handling the yacht they would not be paid. In spite of our agents saying they had been presented with a large stevedoring bill, they accepted that it was a try-on and it was never paid.

On arrival in Mombasa the ship was berthed in the stream at the top of the harbour. The ship's derricks discharged the harbour tug and then *Tresca* was gently offloaded alongside and a Southern Engineering launch towed her to our workshop. We gave Captain Martin a slap-up dinner and he said it had been the most worrying trip he had ever undertaken in case the chairman's yacht was damaged in any way.

While in England I made contact with Charles Nicholson of Camper & Nicholson, the yacht builders, who supplied me with two large pieces of silver spruce to repair the mast. Southern Engineering built wooden trestles on which the mast was laid. When the spruce arrived the doubtful section was cut out and the new pieces scarfed in. The great day came when the mast was ready to be stepped. There was another vessel alongside Southern Engineering with a reasonably high derrick. A large gang of Southern Engineering workers lifted the mast and carried it alongside, a strop was put round the mast and it was carefully hoisted into an upright position, over the slot in *Tresca's* deck. The heel was gently lowered through the slot and into the boat until it fitted into the appropriate position over the keel. Everyone's worry, including my own, was the possibility of a vessel making a wash big enough to cause *Tresca* to roll. However, all went well and everything coupled up and the new stainless steel shrouds proved to be the exact length. The main boom was fitted and the sails bent on. We took *Tresca*, under power, around the main harbour and then hoisted the mainsail and jib and sailed into Port Reitz and out to sea for a run. She sailed beautifully. After the run we berthed her alongside at Southern Engineering and there she stayed, having an internal refit organised by Margaret, with occasional trips, until February 1969 when we decided to sail to Aldabra Island in the Seychelles and back, a distance of over 2,000 miles.

John Worsley and girlfriend flew out to join us on the trip and John Williams and Jane Bainbridge, Dick's daughter, came down from Nairobi as part of the crew. We had two Bajuni Arabs from Lamu as our permanent crew. Margaret loaded stores to last at least a month and off we sailed, with Dick Bainbridge accompanying us out of the Mombasa entrance in his yacht, named *Malaika* (angel) after the popular local song. We headed for Aldabra Island, with its 23-mile-long lagoon. The only accessible entrance to the lagoon is on the north-west side where there is a deep channel. During the First World War the German cruiser *Königsberg* stopped at Aldabra to take on coal from an accompanying collier. She was only able to get into the northern part of the main channel where she anchored briefly. We took our inflatable boat, with an outboard, from the western entrance and slowly explored some of the many creeks. The bird life was quite incredible and the sooty terns when nesting in the mangroves could be held gently in one's hand, their only reaction being to peck. The island is inhabited by the world-famous giant tortoises. During the day they tend to lie in the sandy areas and where possible the shade of mangroves. If you wanted one

DAILY NOTES AND SKETCHES

One of John Worsley's sketches with which he adorned Tresca's *log book*

to move you scratched its back, which seemed to tickle and it would immediately move off.

After Aldabra we sailed north-east to the Seychelles and anchored in Port Victoria, and then alongside the long quay where we refuelled with diesel and took on fresh water. There is a lovely bay at Beau Vallon on one side of the island and we put in there for a few days. After a week in Mahé the others, who had spent a week ashore, rejoined for the trip back to Mombasa. John Worsley, a first-class artist, made a number of sketches in the log book which we still have. We always chose to sail to the Seychelles and back during the north-west monsoon when the prevailing wind was from the north and at times was so light that we could hardly keep going without using the engine. We usually kept a hooked line trailing astern and invariably caught large fish. Often when reeling in the line a shark would come up and take our catch, leaving just the head to be hauled aboard. The only vessels we ever saw were large tankers fully laden from the Gulf proceeding round the Cape, or else northbound in ballast for the next cargo of crude. Sadly, some of the large tankers in ballast used to clean their tanks at sea, which was strictly illegal, and near some of the islands the bird life was badly affected by oil slicks. Star sights were taken every evening and we sighted land about five miles south of Mombasa.

Over the next few years we frequently dived off the East African coast and the Seychelles to collect shells for Margaret's collection, which became well known in the conchological world. I bought a couple of Aquanauts to help, which consist of a circular yellow tube, about the size of a car tyre, containing an engine-driven compressor and large intake pipe well clear of any exhaust fumes. Fresh air was blown through 30-foot flexible pipes to our backpacks and into a full-face mask. If the mask steamed up we lifted the edge, which allowed water in, then put it back and the water was blown out. A tank of petrol would keep the engine running for an hour and a half. On most days we would find a fish that stayed near us and as we turned a rock the fish would dart down and pick up any succulent morsel. When the engine stopped we would surface and refuel. By the end of the second dive we would be rather exhausted and head for home. It was a fascinating life on the reef and we saw some wonderful fish and occasionally the odd shark would circle us. We were told (whether it is true or not) that if we made a high-pitched noise they would swim away. I found it very easy to make a high-pitched noise when I saw some of these huge sharks!

On a holiday in England in 1969 we visited an old friend of Margaret's, Joan Cliff, who had a small cottage at Pennington near Lymington, Hampshire. This was about the time when Margaret said we ought to buy a property for use during the children's holidays. Joan used Prospect Cottage when visiting her elderly mother in Boldre. On arrival at the cottage, Margaret said to me, 'Go into Lymington and get some wine for dinner, and a bottle of port for you.'

We had an enjoyable dinner with Joan, and afterwards Margaret suggested I have some port. I thought, how nice, and after several glasses Margaret told me Joan wanted to sell the cottage and were we interested in buying it? It was only later, having said yes, I realised that the port had quite a lot to do with it. In those days property prices were fairly low and we bought the cottage for £6,500. Whilst there we went for a drink with Joan's mother in Boldre Lane at a house called The Heritage, with a walled garden and orchard. Little did we realise at the time that we would subsequently also buy this house.

By 1970 we had been in Mombasa for twenty-one years and Dick Bainbridge felt he wanted to retire. We gave him a going-away party with a Seychellois band. After sailing for a time in *Malaika*, Dick, whose health was getting worse, bought a house in Dartmouth overlooking the creek. Dick's chest became so bad that he had to return to the King Edward VII Hospital in Midhurst, where the lobe of his lung was removed. This time cancer of the lung was diagnosed and Dick wrote to me in the Seychelles where he still had a shareholding in Mahé Shipping. He asked me to look after his shareholding until such time as I felt it best to sell. Susan, the second daughter, was getting married and Dick decided that he must leave hospital and return to Dartmouth

Directors of the East Africa National Shipping Line [Tony, top right]

113

for the wedding. Sadly, two days before the wedding Dick died. In Kenya, his death had a full-page coverage written by Edward Rodwell in the *Mombasa Times*, who described Dick as 'one of the world's true gentlemen'. In all our years together we had never had a disagreement and we all missed Dick immensely. Susan married Willie Roberts and continued living in Kenya. Jane, his eldest daughter, married Ian Craig in Kenya where she lives to this day on the Lewa Downs conservancy.

Our next long trip in *Tresca* was in 1971 with Mike Groves and his French wife Odile, Eric Cecil, Basil Bell and Geoffrey Bedford, a director of East Africa National Shipping Line. We anchored off Cosmoledo Island, part of the Seychelles group, on 3 October. The following day, however, while under the pilotage of a local Seychellois manager, we grounded while negotiating a narrow channel into the lagoon. *Tresca* lay over to port during the night but in the early hours refloated and appeared sound. The lagoon had a clear sandy bottom, and to my excitement, dotted around on the bottom were some very large helmet shells. I hurriedly put on my flippers and facemask and dived over the side with the idea of picking one up. I found it was far deeper than anticipated and so got the Aquanaut. I dived down towards a nice big shell and eventually when about four feet above the shell my hose to the Aquanaut became fully stretched and at the same time the little engine was running slower. Stupidly, as the enticing shell was so near I gave an extra kick with my flippers, and as I got my hands on the shell the engine stopped. I started flipping my way to the surface and in the end was seeing stars and realised I could not last much longer. I managed to make the surface and a member of the crew got hold of my line and the shells. When I reached the deck a sounding was taken and we realised we were anchored in ten fathoms or 60 feet.

I sat on deck and stripped the Aquanaut, dispersing the salt water, and eventually got it going. There were still many helmet shells on the bottom and the only way to get them was by a line with a weight on it. With my goggles and flippers I held on to the end of the line that had a weight on it, and the other end was made fast on deck. One breathed in and out about twenty times, known as hyperventilating, took a deep breath, and jumped in holding the weight. This took me straight to the

DAILY NOTES AND SKETCHES

We invariably caught large fish ... but sometimes a shark would take our catch

bottom, where I would let go of the weight, swim quickly to the nearest helmet shell, pick it up and start flipping back to the surface again. In this way I managed to gather about five or six shells, until Margaret said she had sufficient!

We sailed to Astove Island, part of the Aldabra group, where Geoffrey Bedford was collected in our aircraft, flown by Tom James, and taken back to Mombasa. We sailed via Aldabra and eventually anchored off the French satellite tracking station on Isle Glorieuse in the French Comoros, a heavily guarded and protected area.[54] Margaret, having communicated with a minister in France, obtained permission for us to fish and dive for shells. Here again the water was beautifully clear with a sandy bottom. There was a small airstrip on the island on which a Dakota would land every month with supplies and drinking water for the French personnel. The plane had to be manhandled round to taxi back to the other end, and manhandled round again for take-off. The next day the *Lindblad Explorer* arrived and anchored off the island.

One of the officers came over to us in his Zodiac and said, 'What in hell are you doing here?' We told him we had permission and asked him what the problem was. He said, 'We have told all the passengers that we are the first ship to come here as it is a forbidden island, and now people do not believe anything we tell them.' Southern Line were agents for the ship, which was on its maiden voyage around the Indian Ocean islands prior to pioneering the Antarctic and Amazon tourist trade. In 2005 she hit an iceberg and sank, a fitting grave for a stalwart ship. We continued on to the Comoros and in Moroni took a taxi up the road leading to the active volcano, Mount Karthala. All the beaches on Moroni had black sand due to past volcanic action. We returned to Mombasa at the end of November.

13

THE SEYCHELLES

Our acquisition of the house Sans Souci, once the governor's weekend residence in the Seychelles, is quite an amusing story. In 1967 during a visit to the Seychelles, whilst we were still in Kenya, I motored up to Sans Souci. In those days the tarmac ended before the house and became a dirt road where sometimes one had to roll fallen rocks off the road. I drove into Sans Souci through an imposing entrance and down a steeply sloping drive to the main house.

Nothing much had been done to the house since Archbishop Makarios had been exiled there in the 1950s. However, the position of the property was magnificent, 1,000 feet up the La Morne mountain, and if one walked round to the seaward side that looked over the port, one could count twenty-three islands.

The next time I was in England I was invited to a Chamber of Shipping black tie dinner in London at a table next to our brokers, H. E. Moss. On examining the seating plan I noted a member of the Ropner family,

Sans Souci front door

Sans Souci

who owned not only the inter-island ferry between Mahé and Praslin but also Sans Souci. During dinner I mentioned to David Ropner that I had recently been to the Seychelles and understood that they owned the ex-Makarios house. As it was then unoccupied I said, 'Do you want to sell it?' He said, 'Do you want to buy it?' I said, 'Have you ever been to the house?' He said, 'No.' I said, 'It is in a terrible condition and if you give it to me I might take it over.'

After dinner David Ropner said, 'Drop me a line over Seychelles', and we went home. Before I left London I had an exchange of telexes with Ropner's that ended with my final offer of £7,500, which to my amazement they accepted.

In the mid-1950s Cyprus was the centre of a fierce conflict between EOKA and British troops.[55] Archbishop Makarios was seen to have an affiliation with EOKA and was deported to Mahé in March 1956, and housed at Sans Souci together with the Bishop of Kyrenia. With nothing to occupy their lives, they sat on a large rock every evening overlooking the edge of the garden and sang.[56] People down on the edge of the town would stop in the road and listen to these melodious voices singing their Greek songs. Some years later when I eventually met Makarios in Cyprus I mentioned the story of their singing, and that in the undergrowth by the rock we had found a large pile of empty champagne bottles. Makarios had a great sense of humour and said, 'Now you realise why we sang so well.' During their incarceration they were given a bottle of champagne a day by the British government.

In 1969 when we were staying with friends, Paddy and Ken Dancy, in Cyprus, there was a call from Makarios's secretary to call on him. When I arrived at the presidential palace the next morning I was ushered into his study. There was no preamble, the secretary merely said, 'Thank you for coming along, his beatitude would like to purchase your house in the Seychelles.'

As an opening salvo, I said an American had offered me over £50,000. He said, 'Never sell to an American.' I consolidated my position by saying £50,000 is neither here nor there to me for my wife's happiness. The preamble being over, we were shown into Makarios's palatial room. After a little small-talk, Makarios said that if I were interested in selling my house in the Seychelles he would be keen to make an offer. His secretary said, 'It is no good talking to him, your beatitude, it is his wife we have to work on.'

I first flew to the Seychelles from Mombasa in our twin Comanche with Margaret, and Tom James as co-pilot, in March 1971, before the airfield was completed. I telephoned the person who would be the first Air Traffic Controller in Seychelles and arranged that if I flew over the airport on arrival the workmen would be cleared off the runway, leaving sufficient room to land a small aircraft. However, I was unable to obtain clearance to fly direct to Mahé, and had to go the long route, via Moroni in the Comoros, then on to the Seychelles. The total flight time for Mombasa–Seychelles was 9 hours 35 minutes. When we arrived, the airfield was duly cleared and I made an easy landing. I explained to the Air Traffic Controller that the leg Moroni–Seychelles was about the same length as Seychelles–Mombasa. However, we had to return the same way.

Coincidentally, I returned to Cyprus later in 1971, at the request of the Seychelles governor Bruce Greatbatch, to join the inaugural commercial BOAC flight to the new airport at Mahé. He considered I should be on the flight due to my connection with the port development in the islands since the aircraft was refuelling in Cyprus.

Earlier that year I had been the first to land on the new airfield. To my dismay when I joined the inaugural flight in Cyprus, I found myself sitting next to Jimmy Mancham, who proceeded to recite his poetry ad infinitum.[57] Having landed several times myself in Mahé with our aircraft, I noticed that when landing there always seemed to be a downdraught from the mountain and I wondered how the pilot would handle things. The aircraft touchdown was very bumpy, and then the brakes were slammed on and the pilot applied full reverse thrust, and stopped the aircraft at the far end of the runway just short of the sea. In those days people always seemed to dress in their best clothes, especially for an inaugural flight. Most of the ladies wore hats and about an hour before landing it was difficult to get into the toilets for the titivating that went on.

I flew in our own aeroplane from Mombasa to the Seychelles for the second time in March 1972. On my return flight on 23 March 1972 it was agreed I could return to Mombasa direct, provided I took off just before the Albatross seaplane on its weekly run between Mombasa and Mahé servicing the tracking station. I took off at 07.55, just ahead of the seaplane, which gradually caught up and then pulled ahead. I still had it in sight when Mombasa came into view after a flight time of 5 hours 50 minutes. For any long trip the drill is to take off on main tanks then switch to auxiliaries to check these, and then to wing-tip tanks and stay on these until they are low. On a long trip I used to climb to about 9,000 feet, where the mixture could be leaned out and the propeller pitch altered for an economic cruising speed. Human nature being what it is, whenever I was over the sea the engines used to sound very rough but smoothed out nicely when in sight of land.

Later that year we were attending a shipping meeting in Brussels when we received a telegram from our friend Joan Cliff saying The Heritage in Boldre Lane, Lymington was for sale. An auction price of £27,000 had been set but if we were prepared to pay £30,000 this would clinch the deal. We agreed and bought The Heritage and sold Prospect Cottage for £16,000. A good profit on the £6,500 purchase price three years earlier.

In 1973 Gerry Read of Shell, Nairobi telephoned me to say they required a vessel to supply fuel to the Seychelles, so it was decided Southern Line should purchase a tanker for the route. Moss recommended a small tanker of about 1,000 tons trading in France, which we bought on behalf of Mahé Shipping, a company we had formed the previous year. Gerry and I were at Mahé to welcome her and we renamed her *Spirit of Mahé*. Later that year we purchased the 2,000-ton cargo vessel *Helmi*, which became the third vessel to be named *Southern Isles*.

Spirit of Mahé

In 1974 Margaret and I decided to leave Kenya and settle in the Seychelles. I sold Southern Line to the East African Conference Lines and our personal effects, including Margaret's MGB GT, went in one of our ships to Mahé. Before selling the company, we took on Captain James Harwood, who had worked for the railways and harbours in Mombasa. His wife, Rosemary, had asked Margaret whether the company could take James on as he was not getting on well with the manager of the port handling services. We agreed and then wondered how best to employ him. He was tasked with making cargo stowage plans for the National Line ships but our agency department found he was only really needed for half the time. I offered to take him to the Seychelles to work for Mahé Shipping in the port. On the termination of his railways and harbours appointment he commuted his pension and invested in shares. When he joined Mahé Shipping, Rosemary insisted that she would only stay for a year, which was the initial agreement. When we took possession of Sans Souci I put James in the house, as Mahé Shipping had to either give him a housing allowance or accommodate him. With the opening of the new port James used to go in each morning with Alfred Lablache, the General Manager of Union Lighterage, and arrange the stevedoring for the day. At the end of James's first year Rosemary agreed to stay for another year and James then asked whether he would be pensionable. This was a problem because our normal pension was 5 per cent contribution by the employee and 5 per cent by the company, and this we realised was no use for a year's employment. We therefore decided to top up James's pension, with him paying 5 per cent and 15 per cent by the company. He was also made officer-in-charge of the pension fund. At the end of the second year James was made a director of Mahé Shipping and he and Rosemary were given a lovely house at the north end of the island at North End Point.

On arrival in the Seychelles we moved into Sans Souci and quickly found the white ants had had a marvellous time. Margaret got in touch with a friendly architect and with the original plans and some photographs, asked him to prepare a design for the house. There was a wooden pillar in the main bedroom and I was asked to knock a nail in it for a small mirror. One tap of the hammer sent the nail in up to its head and the pillar very quickly came down. Margaret had a flair for making a house attractive and we set about rebuilding it with a local Seychellois foreman, a gang of workmen and a carpenter named François. He turned out to be a wonderful carpenter who seldom appeared on a Monday when he was recovering from a monumental hangover. As the house took shape it became apparent that the new house would be nothing like the plans, so these were scrapped and we reverted to the image of the old Sans Souci, including the corrugated iron roof. We started off with a guest wing on one side of the house, an extension of the garage with its own glass sliding doors on to the garden, with a bath and shower facing the other way, which we lived in during the two-year reconstruction. The front of the house had a tiled patio with a small round lily pond. Beyond this was the main entrance to the house. Before leaving Kenya we had purchased timber from Steel Bros in Lindi and the best pieces were stored in the Southern Line office in Mombasa, including two large pieces of teak, each about 3 feet wide and 7.5 feet long. These were taken to Lamu where an Arab carpenter carved out two magnificent doors to form the main entrance. There were large brass studs on the door, the origin of which date back to India to prevent elephants knocking the door down. The lintel was heavily carved and included both our initials in Arabic.

Some years previously Southern Line had bought shares in Wilken Aviation in Nairobi and we knew John Falconer-Taylor, the ex-senior pilot and good friend who had recently emigrated to the Seychelles. He and I felt that we should inaugurate an inter-island air service, between Mahé and Praslin, the next largest island. The government had built a narrow bumpy landing strip on Praslin, which became slippery in the rainy season. We formed a small company, Air Mahé, and were allocated a corrugated hangar at Mahé airport, but had to keep spares in an air-conditioned store due to the humidity. The service to Praslin, with Britten-Norman Islander aircraft ferried from Kenya by John, proved very popular and we were approached by Robert Delorie, owner of Bird Island, a breeding ground for thousands of seabirds, to put in a small strip. John considered it would be quite expensive, as we would have to do it ourselves, and we would require a lighter with the necessary mechanical equipment including a bulldozer and roller for compacting the airstrip. I had a chat with Robert Delorie and he promised us that as he owned most of Bird Island, we would be given sole rights to fly there. I told John we should have a written undertaking from Robert giving Air Mahé the sole right but he laughed and said we must trust his word. We knew the Seychellois promises were of little value and so it proved to be. I remember it cost us some £5,000, which in those days seemed quite a lot of money. After a few months Robert Delorie was approached by an Italian who went on to run the service from Mahé to Bird Island. Bird Island was a lovely spot with clear blue sea and sandy beaches and the food they provided was delicious. There were little overnight bandas (huts) with mosquito nets surrounding the beds and the birds would perch on the windowsills and roof beams. There was no malaria in the Seychelles but mosquitoes came out in droves around sunset. A few years later, when air services started from Madagascar to Mahé, all aircraft had to be sprayed before landing, as dengue fever, which had arrived from Kenya, was rife in Madagascar. Both Margaret and I had a bad attack. It starts with a headache and high temperature and bleeding. The sad thing about it is that it mutates and can return in various forms. This is carried by the *Aedes albopictus* mosquito which is different to the malarial *Anopheles* type.[58]

Mahé Shipping Company, registered in 1973, had several of the main shipping agencies, and the stevedoring, loading and discharge of the ships was by rusty old lighters provided by the Union Lighterage Company, a local company with Asian directors. I remember when the airport was being built a Dutch company had the contract financed by Britain. At the time I was still the Seychelles government representative in East Africa and became a great friend of Bruce Greatbatch, the then governor, who was knighted during his tenure of office.[59] Whenever I visited the Seychelles from Mombasa I stayed with him at Government House.

In 1974 the port working was archaic, with cargo discharged by ship's derrick into a lighter and towed to the pier. Everything was then manhandled out of the lighter by stevedores putting lines round each crate and hauling it end-over-end to the pier, and again rolling each crate end-over-end and up into the lorries, and breakages were terrible. I said to Bruce Greatbatch we would like to apply to run the new port, if and when completed. He said it was the obvious thing but politically there would be an uproar from the local Asians who ran Union Lighterage. Bruce said the only thing was that Mahé Shipping should buy Union Lighterage, which I thought was a dreadful idea. All their rusty lighters were obsolete and their organisation and management were deplorable. Bruce was quite adamant and insisted that he could not advise the British government on port renovation unless we bought the company.

I started negotiating with them, saying that Mahé Shipping was interested in buying them out, and, knowing the Asian community, was not surprised when they quoted ridiculous prices. One of their directors, Jimmy Wadia, was the most troublesome. In the end we agreed to take over Union Lighterage, retaining Mr Lablache and Jimmy Wadia as directors. In due course new lighters and mooring boats were ordered from Southern Engineering in Mombasa. I mentioned to Bruce Greatbatch that it was a pity that the Dutch company building the airport had not also been contracted by the British government to build some deepwater berths in the port. Bruce thought this a marvellous idea and eventually the British government gave the Dutch company a new contract to build a deepwater berth long enough to accommodate two vessels.

As construction of the new port proceeded, we built new offices for Union Lighterage and an engineering workshop to service the equipment, including mobile cranes, ships' handling gear and the construction of pallets. There was a firm in Leicester, England which sold refurbished equipment including lathes and milling machines and they supplied everything for the workshops. Just before completion of the port we built over 1,500 new pallets and ran classes to educate the stevedores in the proper handling of cargo and stacking in the sheds. The latter was important since the Seychelles imported a huge quantity of rice and it was essential to stack the bags on pallets after three tiers to give proper ventilation.

On 29 June 1976 Britain gave the Seychelles its independence and a grand ceremony took place at the stadium, where the Duke of Gloucester, whom Margaret and I accompanied on a flight from London, handed over to Jimmy Mancham, the Chief Minister. The opposition party, headed by Albert René, attended the ceremony but as yet had no power in the Legislative Assembly.[60] From then on the Legislative Assembly was run by the new governor, Colin Allan, a New Zealander, under Jimmy Mancham, with David Dale, who had been a colonial minister under the British administration. David stayed on and became secretary to the cabinet. He used to frequently drive up to Sans Souci with his wife Hannah, and spend the evening with us. After a time the opposition in the legislature accused him of being one of our stooges and they wanted to run everything in the port without the involvement of Mahé Shipping. A statement was made that Union Lighterage and the whole port operation were to be nationalised. I flew back to London and met the British minister involved, putting our case that we had been asked by Bruce Greatbatch to run the port in the first place. A considerable amount of money had been spent setting up the port operation, building the office block and the engineering infrastructure, and in the event of nationalisation taking place we would require adequate compensation from the government. In the event the Seychelles government was dissuaded from nationalisation and we were back where we started. London sent out a port advisor named Workman who came to our offices to tell us what experience he had in port operation, and his knowledge of the subject. After a couple of months we realised that Workman's ambition was eventually to take over the port from Mahé Shipping and Union Lighterage and virtually run the port operation himself. Things remained like this for the next nine months but it was obvious that Workman was on the side of the Seychelles government.

Some time before independence in Seychelles a wealthy Arab named Adnan Khashoggi arrived in his own large jet aircraft, together with his entourage.[61] A few days later his personal motor yacht arrived with an English captain and crew. He took the various ministers for a trip round the island and then they were offered a sightseeing trip in his aircraft and everyone was presented with a diamond-studded watch. Khashoggi told Jimmy Mancham that he wished to invest in a big way in Seychelles, and to this end bought a large tract of land at Trois Frères.

In 1977 a Commonwealth Conference was set up in London attended by President Mancham and all his ministers. Jimmy was to make the opening speech as the newest member of the Commonwealth, when Albert René, the head of the opposition party, took the opportunity to stage a Communist coup. David Dale, as secretary to the cabinet, was immediately summoned by Jimmy, who was staying at the Savoy Hotel. Khashoggi asked Jimmy to meet him in Paris and on his arrival with David Dale, Khashoggi announced that an aircraft full of mercenaries was on standby to fly to the Seychelles in a counter-coup. There was a stipulation that Jimmy would follow a few hours later and announce his return as head of government. Sadly, Jimmy was reluctant to accept the challenge.

I was in England at the time of the coup and considered that I should return as soon as possible. I took the first flight to Mahé on British Airways and found there was only one other passenger travelling with me in first class. He was very pleasant and I knew he was trying to find out why I was on the aeroplane.

In the end he asked me point blank my reasons for going out to the island. When told I was chairman of a number of companies on Mahé, he heaved a sigh of relief and told me that the purpose of his trip was to try and obtain the contract for a new currency. He worked for Perkins Bacon, the banknote printers.

As the Seychelles was very much in the news at that moment I was seen by Margaret on BBC TV news walking down the aircraft steps to face the music – so to speak. I was met by James Harwood, who took me straight to Sans Souci and said he was forbidden to work in the office until further notice. This I ignored and went down in my car to the office that afternoon. My office on the first floor looked across to the police station, which was full of new ministers along with the new chief of police. That evening I telephoned the man from Perkins Bacon and invited him to dinner at the Tartaruga Felice, an Italian restaurant. We sat at a veranda table and at the table next to us were a couple of the new regime ministers. They were whispering together and I realised they were discussing us. One of them, alluding to me, whispered that I was a Jew. This was too much. I stood up, went over to him and said, 'I am not a Jew, I am a Roman Catholic', whereupon they both left the restaurant!

Over the next few days things seemed to quieten down. Initially René was obviously very worried and expecting a counter-coup any time. My banknote friend and I returned on the same flight to London with the addition of the author Wilbur Smith, who had property on Long Island, close to Mahé. The situation gradually simmered down until Jimmy Mancham contacted me again saying that they had now decided to undertake a counter-coup and all was ready to go, with the exception of the money. I told Jimmy that although I was sympathetic to him, I was not going to be a financial provider, but promised to see what I could do. I telephoned my old friend Jack Weatherill, who was then Speaker of the House of Commons, and he invited me to lunch.

Over lunch I explained the situation in Seychelles and when we came to the coffee he said, 'There is Richard Luce over there, let me get hold of him.'[62] He joined us and I again explained the position and he was most enthusiastic and said that I would receive a letter from No. 10 Downing Street within a week or two. Sure enough, two weeks later I received a letter from No. 10 saying that it had been arranged for me to meet Richard Luce in the Foreign Office. In due course I appeared in this morgue of a building and approached an elderly lady at reception, giving my name and saying that I had an appointment with Mr Luce. She looked through her notebook and said, 'Ah, yes', and picked up the telephone. A young man appeared, shook me by the hand and said, 'Hello, Mr Bentley-Buckle, I have the Seychelles desk. I have only had it for a couple of months and I am afraid the only thing I know about Seychelles is where it is.'

We proceeded down the long corridor and in another room appeared another secretary, this time Richard Luce's. The three of us went to the minister's door. Richard Luce was immaculately dressed, had a weak handshake and asked what he could do for me. First I stated that I must have their assurances that anything discussed in his office would not leave the building and that I was not prepared to say anything further unless I received this assurance. Richard Luce said this was perfectly all right, and I told him all I knew about the proposed counter-coup and the requirement for further funds. Luce said that whilst the British government would welcome a return to the previous government, they could in no way be seen to be involved. I thanked him and said I would not waste any more of his time. As I walked to the door he put a piece of paper in my hand saying I suggest you telephone this number. This I did, only to find it was the American Embassy, and the next morning I paid them a visit. The reception there was completely different. They said, 'Leave it to us, but you must put us fully in the picture.' I gave them Jimmy Mancham's London address and telephone number and left. The US were very suspicious of a possible Russian presence in the Indian Ocean, especially as they had a large air and naval base at the Diego Garcia archipelago.

On 25 November 1981 the counter-coup took place. It was organised by some Seychellois in South Africa and led by Mike Hoare. The mercenaries called themselves the 'Froth Blowers' and they were to visit the Seychelles ostensibly on a beer-drinking and golfing spree. They duly arrived at the airport and their luggage was given a cursory examination. As they started to board a bus, a woman customs officer tried to move some of the luggage across the counter. It proved so heavy she immediately demanded that it be opened for a complete examination. The mercenary in question ran to the waiting bus shouting, 'It's all over chaps, get your toys out', and then boarded the bus which took off at speed down the road towards the military barracks situated outside the airport perimeter fence at the end of the runway. The mercenaries stopped any movement from the barracks and took over the airport. As this happened, an Air India flight was due to land in Seychelles for refuelling. Air Traffic Control contacted the flight and told it to divert to another airport. Although all flights are supposed to retain sufficient fuel for such a diversion, Air India had only taken on enough fuel to land at Seychelles, where the price was cheaper, and the plane had insufficient to divert, so it duly landed. The Froth Blowers, still holding the airport, forced the Air India flight to refuel then boarded and ordered the pilot to fly to Durban. That was the end of the hoped-for counter-coup and occasionally one would see a small sign in the back window of a car that read, 'Another shitty day in paradise', but no one took any notice. Life must go on and after four years of the struggle and tedium of living under a Communist regime we sat up one day and said, 'What on earth are we doing living here?'

14

ROUND THE WORLD

When Dick and I were shareholders in Bunson Travel in Kenya, the directors agreed that we should also form Bunson Travel (Seychelles) Ltd, which was granted an IATA licence. When British Airways crews came to Seychelles and had time off, we gave them trips with Air Mahé to Pralin and Bird Island. As a result British Airways gave me a 90 per cent rebate on first-class trips and a 75 per cent rebate for Margaret. We looked through the various Wexas Travel brochures and, with our rebates, I found that we could travel by air round the world, providing we continue in one direction, for a total cost of £3,000. Consequently, as some of the Mahé Shipping vessels were registered in the Cayman Islands for convenience, we arranged that Geoffrey Bedford and Rupert Brennecke, who were directors of the company, should meet us there.

We set off in January 1981 via Sri Lanka, where I met my sister Pat and her husband George Hayley. George's family had a trading company, Hayley's, which had been trading on the island since the 19th century. We visited temples and shrines and a sanctuary with elephants before going on to Trincomalee, where Dick and I had bought our first motor fishing vessel and started our adventures which led to the formation of Southern Line. From there we flew to Hong Kong and met up with many East African friends, including Anne and Anton Jansen, who had taken on our two pug dogs when we left Kenya, with the promise that they would not put them into quarantine. When Anne and Anton moved to Hong Kong, the dogs were shipped to Hong Kong on a Dutch East African Line ship and smuggled ashore at night in a sampan. On seeing us the dogs gave us a terrific welcome, refusing to move off our laps. Our next stop was San Francisco, where we stayed with Peggy Guttard, who also had property in the Seychelles. We drove south to Los Angeles and visited the Hollywood Studios and the Walk of Fame pavement with paving stones studded with names of famous stars. We stayed downtown in the Beverley Wilshire Hotel.

When the time came to leave the hotel our luggage was deposited in the foyer with the head porter, who was a large man in a grey morning suit and top hat. I slipped him five dollars and said, 'Could you get us a taxi to the airport?' 'Ja, ja,' he replied. I said, 'You are not an American, are you?' 'No,' he replied. I asked him, 'Could you be German?' He replied, 'Ja.' I said, 'Ich kann auch etwas Deutsch sprechen, ich war Kriegsgefangener im letzten Krieg.' (I can also speak some German, I was a prisoner of war in the last war.) He replied, 'Wo waren Sie?' I said, 'Ich war in einem Marinelager zwischen Bremen und Hamburg.' 'Mensch,' he said, 'Westertimke.' He turned to me and said, 'My uncle was in charge of security there.' I asked him his uncle's name, to which he replied, 'Oberleutnant Schoof', who of course was one of the Gestapo officers in the camp who had slipped away at the end of the war. I turned to him and said, 'Give me back my five dollars', but I never got it back.

We flew to the Caymans in the West Indies, a relaxing venue for a Mahé Shipping board meeting, where we met Geoffrey and his wife Maureen together with Rupert and his daughter. With business done, we flew south to Rio de Janeiro, a mixture of opulence and slums, and visited the impressive statue of Christ the Redeemer, completed in 1931, which towers over the city and the 200,000-seater football stadium. From here we flew to Buenos Aires, where the central square was a mass of flowering jacaranda trees, and then finally back to Cape Town in March.

Whilst we were there we stayed at the Mount Nelson Hotel and were looked after by our friends Mary and Peter Melck. Over a buffet lunch in the Oasis Restaurant with them and Con and Joyce McGee, I said, 'We ought to buy a place here.' Con said, 'I know just the place for

you.' And I said, 'When could we see it?' Con replied, 'After lunch.' Con had been keen on the place but Joyce, his wife, did not want to know. I asked Con what price Mrs Hodgson was asking for the house and he said he understood it was 140,000 rand, but I could get a special rate if I brought money in from abroad. The price worked out at £52,000 and we could ask the agents when we could inspect the house.

A meeting was arranged with the agent to view the house and Margaret and I arrived, to be met by an elderly lady with her two Alsatian dogs. Her deceased husband, an architect, had designed the house and it was a beautiful building with parquet floors and a huge fireplace in the drawing room. The house was built in Spanish style with 2½ acres of garden. The drawing room led onto a terrace with a water garden and fountain. We discovered that several people had made offers for the house but old Mrs Hodgson kept turning them down. It was March at the time and I said to her, 'Mrs Hodgson, I would like to purchase your house and can put the money down within a week. However, there is a snag, I cannot take over and move in until the end of the year. Would you be prepared to look after the property until then?'

This clinched the deal, as it gave the old lady sufficient time to sort herself out with her two dogs, and that's how we came to buy Fontellas in Monterey Drive, Constantia, Cape Town. We then completed our circumnavigation of the world and returned to the Seychelles, a wonderful experience behind us. It took little time to confirm that the Communist-orientated Seychelles was no longer the place for us, and we looked forward to developing our new property in South Africa. Fortunately the American Embassy leased Sans Souci, with the option to purchase, which they eventually did with payments being paid externally.

We returned to England in the summer of 1981, and stayed in our house, The Heritage. While lunching with friends at the Royal Lymington Yacht Club, I got chatting to a local estate agent, Paul Jackson, and asked if he had any interesting houses on the market. He replied, 'Tony, there is one for you, overlooking the Beaulieu River.' I replied that we did not need another house. However, he told me that the German who owned it was going to Hamburg at the weekend and suggested we went to see it. I agreed and told Margaret I was going to

Gardiners Ground

look at a house for sale in Beaulieu. Margaret replied, 'You silly arse, we do not need another house and I am not coming.'

On the Sunday morning, as I was leaving, Margaret said, 'Well, I suppose I had better come with you.' We arrived at Gardiners Ground on a lovely morning with a high tide, and after a cursory inspection returned to The Heritage. Margaret stayed awake quite late after we had gone to bed, saying, 'Are you listening to me?' I replied, 'Yes, dear.' She said, 'I know by that tone of voice you are not listening to a word I am saying. If you miss this house you will regret it to the end of your life.'

The view from the house down river was superb. It was on the market for £275,000, which I considered too high. I telephoned Paul Jackson with an offer of £240,000 including curtains and carpets. He informed me that he had received a far higher offer. I said, 'It is your commission, take it.' Paul told me the people who had put in a higher offer could not complete as quickly as us since I had offered cash. I said, 'Well, too bad, my offer stays open until 4 p.m. on Friday afternoon in three weeks' time.'

Paul kept telephoning me and I continually advised him he had wasted another telephone call, my offer still stood. On the Friday morning three weeks later Paul telephoned and said, 'Tony, Herr Koenig is coming to my office at 3 p.m. this afternoon. If you were able to offer £5,000 lower than the sale price I think I might be able to persuade Herr Koenig to take a deal.' I replied, 'Paul, you have wasted another telephone call.' However, at 4 p.m. in the afternoon Paul phoned and said, 'Tony, I am pleased to tell you I have persuaded Herr Koenig to accept your offer.' Which is how we bought Gardiners Ground. The sale was completed in December 1981.

We returned to Cape Town and moved into Fontellas, where we carried out a number of alterations and built a swimming pool. During our stay June Burton, a South African friend, came to stay and one evening we invited a long-term friend of hers, Pam Golding, for a drink. Pam was a high-powered estate agent who told us of a place for sale that she thought we would like. Margaret was never happy in Fontellas and felt it had an unpleasant atmosphere. The following day we went to see the property, a Dutch thatched farmhouse built in 1813 named Rust en Vrede (Rest and Peace). The house appealed to Margaret and, as I left to join one of our ships, I said I would only be away a week. I then flew to Aden and joined our tanker.

I was sitting with Guy Adam, the skipper, in his cabin one evening when the radio officer came in and said to me, 'A message for you, sir.'

Rust en Vrede (Rest and Peace), Cape Town, South Africa

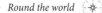

I picked up a signal that said, 'Contact your wife urgently over new house.' On arrival at Hodeidah I immediately called on Abdul Wasa, our agent, and said, 'Abdul, can I telephone my wife?' He said, 'Mr Buckle, sit down and make yourself at home, where do you want to call her?' I said, 'I have got the number in Cape Town.' Abdul said, 'I am very sorry, we are not allowed to telephone South Africa due to apartheid.'

I had to fly back to Cape Town via Nairobi and spent a night at the Muthaiga Club. As I entered, Ali, the long-term factotum at the desk, said, 'Jambo bwana Buckle, habari ya siku mingi' (what news after so long) – there is a telephone call for you.' It was Margaret, saying, 'When are you coming back, you will love the new house, and Pam has completed the agreement for us.'

On my return Margaret handed me the agreement she had been asked to sign by Pam and the sale was agreed shortly after. Fontellas went to auction and sold for a good profit. We had to undertake extensive repairs to Rust en Vrede. There were no foundations other than the large kopje stones on which it was built, and no damp course. The walls were at least two feet thick with sash windows and interior pine shutters. At the end of summer, with the coming of the first rain, there were trickles through the ceiling and roof. We were told the best thatcher was a Mr Adrianse, whose family were ex-slaves from St Helena, an island in the South Atlantic. He arrived with his two sons, full of bonhomie, and told us that we would need a minimum of three weeks' work on areas of the thatch. The house was a historical listed building and the only surviving E-shaped house in the Cape Province. An addition had been made to one end of the E, which had been covered with a corrugated iron roof which leaked. We pulled off the corrugated roof and put in new wooden beams and a thatched roof.

At the time of writing, in 2009, we have owned the house for approximately twenty-eight years and every year Mr Adrianse came to see us. He must have had a good sense of humour, as he was always smiling, and each year on arrival he said, 'Mr Buckle, the price of thatch has gone through the roof this year', whereupon we would bargain until he knew he could get no more out of me. Over the years we have replaced most of the timber beams and the whole of the roof. At the back of the house is an outside wooden staircase to an apple loft in which the wooden floor had rotted away and we completely replaced the floor with Australian jarrah hardwood. To stop the damp, the main outer walls had holes drilled at regular intervals and injected with a silicon compound to seal the damp, which cost about £8,000. Until recently I spent most of the day in the garage where I had a small lathe and most of my tools that I had brought, first from Kenya to the Seychelles and then to Cape Town. I renewed several sash windows, the odd shutter and some of the floors. Although Margaret calls it a labour of love, the love side has now expired! The first year we considered a swimming pool was a must and we built a 10 by 4 metre pool heated by a heat pump. From the stable door at the back of the house to the terrace by the pool we planted four grapevines. On the terrace is a table for eight persons and throughout the summer we have our lunch under the grapevine. I also had breakfast on the terrace after swimming my usual twenty lengths in the pool. We now have a first-class coloured man, Leon Louw, who is a general factotum and keeps everything in good order. In 2006 we decided to transfer the ownership of Rust en Vrede to Deborah, although we pay all the costs as we use it as a second home when we visit South Africa. Margaret's middle sister Hazel and her husband Jeremy Heale lived in a house near Lanseria airport outside Johannesburg. Over the years several squatter camps appeared nearby and Hazel felt that life would soon become intolerable. She decided the best thing to do was to sell their house and move to Cape Town. They now live not far from Rust en Vrede, in a house overlooking Hout Bay on the east side of the Cape peninsula.

15

GARDINERS GROUND

O ur present home, Gardiners Ground, is an imposing building overlooking the Beaulieu River, built in 1933 by Mr and Mrs Penn-Gaskell. During the Second World War an air raid shelter was built on the side of the house, and Herr Koenig, the previous owner, later turned this into a sauna. On 26 May 1942 a string of bombs was dropped around 4 p.m. by a German aircraft, one of which landed on Dock Lane and another on the corner of the kitchen, and Mrs Penn-Gaskell, who was upstairs in the bathroom was thrown out of her bath. Over the years we have made a few alterations. There had been a grass tennis court, which we replaced with a fenced hard court. But really the best thing we put in was a flat. Down the passage on the first floor was a haul-down ladder that led to the loft, which took up the whole of the roof area. Nicholas and Deborah installed a small snooker table. On one occasion Margaret said, 'One day when we are old we will need someone to look after us, and the house.'

We therefore contacted an architect named Hugh Wilkinson to prepare plans for a flat in the loft and he indicated that if we pushed the end wall of the house out by six feet beyond the kitchen we could have a rear entrance, with stairs going up to a flat. The flat would have a sitting room with dining area, a fully equipped kitchen and a corridor to a bathroom. At the end of the corridor would be a double bedroom. We approved the plans and gave the go-ahead. The end result is a very pleasant flat that was initially used as accommodation for friends when they came to stay, but is now occupied by our housekeeper, Carol King, and her husband Ken, who have been with us eleven years in 2009. Numerous workmen were involved in the construction and an alarm was fitted between the kitchen and the house. One day it was found that the back door into the kitchen had been forced and much of the wine had been stolen, including three cases of vintage port, together with a great deal of Belgian pewter. Margaret had always said, 'That dreadful pewter – send it to the local auction house.' Happily the pewter, having been stolen, was taken to Phillips the auctioneers in London by a local family, who were notorious thieves around Beaulieu. Phillips informed the police that the pewter had been valued at just over £1,000. Margaret suggested we clean it and keep it. Kitchen brassware was also stolen but the police recovered it all, with the exception of one nice Indian piece, and we received compensation from our insurance company. The Indian piece was eventually traced to a public house on the Solent. Unfortunately, as the insurance had already paid us £100, we could not claim it back and it is still there to this day, chained to a shelf.

White Otter of Beaulieu, *Moonen 68*

The previous owner of Gardiners Ground, Herr Koenig, had a picture of his sailing yacht with a cloverleaf painted on it. I telephoned Rupert Brennecke, a Kenyan friend in Germany, and asked him if he could throw any light on Koenig. He said the clover-leafed yacht was owned by Koenig, who ran a string of boutiques around Hamburg but had moved to Denmark. One thing we inherited was a copious number of second-hand golf balls. Koenig had practised golf in the garden and we found them in flowerbeds, bushes and the riverbank.

Having sold *Tresca* in the Seychelles in 1984, we bought a Birchwood TS37 motor yacht at the Southampton Boat Show, which we named *White Otter*. We cruised the Solent, the north coast of France, the Bay of Biscay and through the endless locks of the Canal du Midi in the south of France and then on to Mallorca. Five years later we sold her and in June 1989 purchased a Birchwood TS44 motor yacht, which was also named *White Otter of Beaulieu*. We again delivered her to Mallorca, but very soon moved her to Corfu, Greece and onto Kuşadasi, Turkey, where she remained until we sold her in 1995 to the Mayor of Ankara for cash. We counted every note, at his behest, and found it £40 short! The last family yacht we owned was a 68-foot Dutch-built Moonen motor yacht, also named *White Otter*, which I bought in April 1995.

One memorable trip we had with our friends, the Balmes, was from Southampton to Brixham, where we spent the night, and the next day we went on to the Scilly Isles. We arrived in the evening and Margaret and I felt we would like to continue to the south coast of Ireland. The Balmes did not wish to join us so we split up and Margaret and I and our deckhand, who called himself the Skipper, left two days later on a foggy morning and arrived that evening just off Waterford. The next day we motored to Waterford where we spent two days shopping, including buying food, and then headed west along the south coast and arrived at Dungarven, where Margaret had been in touch with our friends Margaret and Martin Miller-Williams, whom we had met in Turkey. Our friends liked the idea of joining us on our yacht and they arrived a couple of days later. We sailed to Crosshaven and picked up a berth in the local yacht yard. Margaret had seen a butcher's shop on the road above the yard and she asked me to go ashore and purchase some beef. The butcher was a very Irish, plump man, who greeted me with, 'Good morning to you, are you enjoying your holiday in Ireland?' I was taken aback and replied, 'Yes, very much.' 'Your first visit to Ireland?' he asked. 'Yes,' I replied, 'I should have come before, as my father was born in County Mayo.' 'Was he now,' said the butcher. I said, 'Yes, and my great-grandfather was the Bishop of Limerick.' 'Glory be to God,' he said, 'I will give you a nice piece of steak.'

A little way down the coast from Crosshaven was the Royal Cork Yacht Club. We hired a car and called there but found it was rather snooty. The mooring was about three times the cost of the Crosshaven mooring, so the next day we sailed to Kinsale.

We had the telephone number of the Watsons, who had been with us when we made our trip over the Karakoram Highway on the Silk Route into China in 1986. We telephoned them and they said come to lunch, and gave us Irish directions. Having taken the wrong road twice, we eventually arrived at the correct turning. The road to their house was at least a mile and a half long, and we eventually arrived at a beautiful old house with a smaller house behind it. The old house they had given to their son, and the Watsons were living in the smaller one. We apologised for being so late and they replied, 'That is nothing, you are in Ireland now.' They gave us an excellent lunch.

The next day we sailed out of Kinsale past the Fastnet Rock and arrived in Crookhaven, where we dropped anchor on the northern side of the entrance. Crookhaven is a long narrow bay and on the southern side just near the entrance was a public house. Our skipper/deckhand went across in the dinghy for some cigarettes and also had a pint and chatted with the locals. He was informed that during the war U-boats used to put into the port and the crews were given food and water by the locals. After this the crews were wished well and went on their way. The south coast of Ireland is full of lovely little creeks and harbours and one could have gone on cruising there for weeks. However, we decided that we must end our trip and return to Beaulieu.

Having cruised around much of the south coast, we decided to move *White Otter* to the Mediterranean in 1996, mooring her in Gibraltar, where we also bought a flat overlooking the marina, Queensway Quay.

The following year Don and Pam Richardson, my daughter-in-law's parents, joined us and we cruised up the Douro River in Portugal. We enjoyed it so much that we returned again in 1998 with Martin and Margaret Miller-Williams.

Unfortunately during this trip I became concerned with the conduct of both the skipper and the deckhand. The skipper was permanently pissed so upon our return to Gibraltar I bought an air ticket for his return to England. Margaret and I were also committed to fly back to England, so we left, leaving the deckhand in charge. We returned to Gibraltar two weeks later, whereupon the deckhand announced his departure.

No sooner had he left than a pleasant Cornish gentleman who moored his boat in the same marina approached me. He said, 'Have you checked your fuel?' I indicated that I had not as I had filled both tanks before I had left. He suggested I check again, which we both did, only to find the tanks were almost empty. Our newfound friend had witnessed a yacht come alongside and the deckhand transfer fuel between the two vessels. Hence the rapid departure of the deckhand.

Margaret, alas, stood with arms akimbo and said, 'I have put up with your bloody boats for thirty-six years, it's either me or the boat.' As we were now without a skipper and a deckhand, and as *White Otter* was too large to manage on our own, we decided to sell her. I arranged for a delivery crew to take her back to Holland, where she was sold in 2000.

Our travels were not just confined to boats. After our round-the-world trip in 1981 we journeyed to the 'roof of the world' in 1986, travelling from Islamabad in Pakistan along the silk route of Cathay, through the Himalayas, Karakoram and the Pamir mountains, to the edge of Mongolia and then flying on to Hong Kong, Thailand and Singapore. A fabulous trip – China was fascinating but the bureaucracy left me with no desire to return.

The following year we travelled to Jordan, up to Jerusalem, Qumran and back to Petra. In 1988 I went to India with Margaret's old school friend Anne Trace.

We resumed our travels again in 1990 to Madagascar, and in 1991 to Namibia and Madeira. In 1992 we travelled to Australia, Fiji, Samoa, Tonga, Hawaii and Los Angeles and back to London.

Whilst we kept our boat in Turkey between 1991 and 1995 we also travelled extensively throughout the Turkish hinterland, the most fascinating and amazing part of the world. The underground cities are mind-boggling and very little is known of their origins.

Between March and April 1994 we flew from Cape Town to Singapore, on to Sabah, Malaysia then Sulawesi in Indonesia and Bali. We then travelled 1,000 miles by road through Java and on to Singapore, from there flying to Hawaii, Los Angeles and back to London.

One of our most memorable trips was in 1996, when we spent three weeks on the *Lindblad Explorer* (a ship I referred to in Chapter 12), when we travelled up the Amazon river, from the mouth as far as Iquitos, a fascinating journey. From Iquitos we then flew on to Chile to visit Machu Picchu.

This in the end was my final trip, but Margaret had one last adventure with our granddaughter Georgina, then eleven years old. Between November and December 2003 they flew from London to Madrid and on to Buenos Aires. After a brief stay they flew to Ushuaia, Tierra del Fuego, where they boarded the MV *Andrea* bound for Antarctica, South Georgia and the Falkland Islands, eventually returning to Ushuaia.

We kept the flat in Gibraltar for a few years and eventually sold it in 2002, when we finally settled into comfortable retirement in Beaulieu. This allowed us more time to spend with the grandchildren, and winters with Deborah in Cape Town.

Once when Jane Craig was staying I asked her when Kiddo died. To my amazement she said Kiddo was still alive and in a residential care home at Liss near Petersfield. I wanted to see her but Jane said, 'I would not if I were you because she may not recognise you.'

I worked out Kiddo was now aged ninety-two years. However, I felt I ought to go because she and I were very close in the old days. On 24 November 2005 Nicholas kindly drove me to Liss to see Kiddo. We arrived to find a nice building, with a number of girls bustling around, and asked to see Mrs Stead. One of them took us to a pleasant airy room looking out on to the garden and it was a great shock to see Kiddo. I would never have recognised her. When I told her who I was, and Nicholas was my son, there was no sign of any recognition. However, when I asked her if she remembered Dick she said, 'Oh yes.'

I spoke to Kiddo about her boat *Orestes*, which she had inherited on the death of her husband, during the war, and she described it as a lovely boat with her nice cabin, which was quite true. After about half an hour I asked her if she remembered Tony and she replied, 'Oh yes I do.' I could see that she did not associate me with Tony, although I said, 'Kiddo, I am Tony.' She replied, 'Oh yes,' but I knew that it did not sink in.

At noon the staff brought in her lunch and I gave her a kiss and we left. While we were at the care home, Kiddo stared at the television, and Nicholas and I realised she was not taking much in, but funnily enough something clicked. I mentioned Eileen Jolly at Shelly Beach Hotel in Likoni, and she smiled and said 'Smelly beach!' which is what we all used to call it – so something did come back.

So much for old age, which Margaret always calls 'a bugger'.

ENDNOTES

1. Two shillings and six pence, half a crown, or 12½ pence in decimal currency.

2. A *Hawkins*-class heavy cruiser built at Devonport, launched in 1920 and armed with 7.5-inch guns. In 1930 *Frobisher* was reduced to reserve before being converted to a Cadet Training Ship, in which role she served from 1932 until 1939.

3. Built between 1916 and 1918, *Vindictive* was designed as a *Hawkins*-class heavy cruiser but underwent many conversions. In 1936–37 *Vindictive* was converted to a training ship for cadets, the work involving the removal of two sets of machinery and the after funnel, and the construction of deckhouses for classrooms for 200 cadets.

4. 'Peace in our time' was the phrase used by Prime Minister Neville Chamberlain on 30 September 1938 (not 1939) after he returned from a meeting with Adolf Hitler, having won Britain another twelve months to prepare for war.

5. A *Danae*-class light cruiser built at Newcastle upon Tyne and launched in 1918. Early in the war she was involved in the hunt for the German battleships *Scharnhorst* and *Gneisenau* after the sinking of the armed merchant cruiser HMS *Rawalpindi*.

6. Vice Admiral Charles Gordon Ramsey who had commanded the destroyer *Acheron* at the Battle of Jutland in 1916.

7. The future Admiral of the Fleet Sir Charles Lambe GCB, CVO (1900–60), who would become First Sea Lord in 1959 and die in office.

8. Admiral Sir Max Kennedy Horton, GCB, DSO** (1883–1951), submarine hero in the First World War, commanded the Northern Patrol at the start of the Second World War, then Flag Officer Submarines, was appointed Commander-in-Chief, Western Approaches in 1942 and was largely responsible for victory in the Battle of the Atlantic.

9. An 11,000-ton, 1,712-passenger, steam turbine ship.

10. *A Man Called Intrepid: The Secret War 1939–1945* by William Stevenson (1976). Stevenson was head of BSC or British Security Coordination in North America during the Second World War. BSC was set up in New York under the leadership of the Canadian industrialist William Stephenson to promote British interests in the USA, counter German propaganda, and help protect shipping from enemy sabotage. The book is mentioned in Nigel West's *Counterfeit Spies: Genuine or Bogus?* (1998) about books of doubtful veracity.

11. *Émile Bertin* was in Halifax, Nova Scotia in June 1940, and was carrying part of the French gold reserves, when France fell to the Germans. The Vichy French government ordered her to Martinique where the gold was unloaded, and she prepared to defend the island against British attack, a plan which was abandoned under United States pressure.

12. The navigation school, HMS *Dryad*, was based in Portsmouth dockyard, but moved to Southwick House when it was taken over from the squire, Robin Thistlethwaite, and

the D-Day landings were planned there. After the war Southwick House was used for teaching navigation, aircraft direction and tactical warfare.

13. On 7 May 1941 with the cruisers *Birmingham* and *Manchester* and the destroyer *Somali*, *Edinburgh* intercepted German weather ship *München* north-east of Iceland, and the German naval code settings, Enigma, for June 1941 were captured. As a result, German naval messages transmitted to U-boats during June 1941 were broken.

14. *Edinburgh* was ordered to intercept *Bismarck* on her projected course for Brest, but *Bismarck* was destroyed on 27 May, and *Edinburgh* was in the Bay of Biscay when she intercepted the German blockade runner SS *Lech* on 28 May 1941.

15. HMS *Repulse* was sunk in the South China Sea in December 1941, with large loss of life.

16. The sub of the gunroom was a job usually given to one of the better, younger officers who would be responsible for discipline, etc. in the junior officers' mess.

17. Rear Admiral Richard Scott (1887–1967) was Rear Admiral, Training Establishments (RATES) based in HMS *Assegai*, Durban from October 1942 to December 1943.

18. Lt Cdr (E) Richard 'Dick' Edward Bainbridge RNVR (1916–1975) was Tony Bentley-Buckle's partner and looked after the engineering side of Southern Line. Born in Bloemfontein South Africa into a family of 13 children, Dick's father had served in the Indian army, and emigrated to South Africa to join the South African Railways. He found it difficult to support his large family and at the age of seven Dick and his elder sister, 'Kiddo', who also appears in these pages, were put on a ship to England to be adopted by a wealthy Aunt. Dick joined the RNVR in September 1941 and served in landing craft during the war. In September 1942 he took part on Operation Agreement, a failed amphibious assault on Tobruk, was wounded in the chest, and sent to Durban to recuperate – where he met Tony Bentley-Buckle. Dick was then sent to the British East Indies fleet where he was mentioned in despatches for his courage, efficiency and devotion to duty in the establishment of navigational aids in the approaches to the Rangoon river, in minesweeping and in the survey of the river prior to Operation Dracula, and he was involved in the preparations for Operation Zipper, the planned landings in Malaya which were forestalled by the dropping of the atom bomb and the surrender of Japan.

19. A six-wheel-drive amphibious truck designed and built by General Motors during the Second World War for transporting goods and troops. The name comes from the builders: D indicates design 1942, U means utility, K indicates all-wheel drive and W indicates two powered rear axles. Commonly called Ducks.

20. Termoli was a small, fortified town and fishing port halfway up the Adriatic coast, north of the spur of the boot of Italy.

21. 'Giles' has not been identified but Farran was Major Roy Alexander Farran DSO, MC** (1921–2006), a British-Canadian soldier, politician, farmer, author and journalist, best known for his exploits with the Special Air Service during the Second World War.

22. Roy Farran, *Winged Dagger: Adventures on Special Service* (1948).

23. Chioggia is a town on a small island about 15 miles south of Venice at the southern entrance to the lagoon of Venice.

24. Lussin Piccolo is a small island off the Dalmatian coast in the Adriatic Sea, some hundred miles south of Trieste, the main port of the old Austro-Hungarian Empire.

25. Guy Morgan, author of *Only Ghosts Can Live* (1945), the title taken from Cecil Day Lewis's poem 'The Conflict': '… Love then with new desires, / For where we used to build and love / Is no man's land, and only ghosts can live / Between two fires.'

26. John Worsley's account of this episode and of life in prisoner-of-war camp is told in *John Worsley's War: An Official War Artist in World War II* by John Worsley and Kenneth Giggal (1993).

27. The Cosulich family were shipowners who originated from Lussin, whose shipping company, Cosulich Line, was nationalised in 1935 by the Italian government. After the war the Cosulich family revived their shipping interests.

28. Lloyd Triestino, founded as Österreichischer Lloyd in 1836, became one of the world's biggest shipping companies, serving the Austro-Hungarian Empire until 1918. The company's name was changed to Lloyd Triestino in 1919, when Trieste became a part of Italy. The company was devastated in the Second World War, losing sixty-eight ships and more than 1,000 sailors, and was reduced to just five ships.

29. Oranienburg concentration camp was established by the Nazis when they gained power in 1933. It held the Nazis' political opponents from the Berlin region, and later was used as a transit camp to the worst hell-holes of the Nazi regime.

30. The Dulags were transit camps through which POWs were sent for sorting and interrogation before being sent to various, more permanent camps.

31. Marlag und Milag Nord was a German prisoner-of-war camp near Westertimke, near Bremen, Germany. Marlag or Marine Lager was for captured British naval personnel and Milag, short for Marineinterniertenlager, was for Merchant Navy personnel.

32. Presumably he means someone who played like Larry Adler.

33. Oberleutnant Schoof was the Camp Security Officer and member of the Gestapo. Oberleutnant is a German army junior officer rank.

34. The Entertainments National Service Association or ENSA was set up in 1939 to provide entertainment for British armed services during the war.

35. Later Air Vice-Marshal James Johnson CB, CBE, DSO** (1915–2001) claimed thirty-four victories over enemy aircraft, seven shared victories, three shared probable, ten damaged, three shared damaged and one destroyed on the ground. Johnson was the highest scoring fighter ace against the German Luftwaffe.

36. Manuel Laureano Rodríguez Sánchez (1917–47), known as Manolete, was gored as he killed the fifth bull of the day in the ring at Linares, east of Córdoba, and died on 28 August 1947, an event which left Spain in a state of shock and El Caudillo, Francisco Franco, ordered three days of national mourning.

37. Navy slang for sleep or a siesta.

38. This is possibly the observer/gunner of the Kingfisher seaplane belonging to HMS *Fidelity*, formerly the French SS *Le Rhin. Fidelity* was a special service vessel on decoy duties manned by Free French, many of whom had taken English names. Sub Lieutenant J. J. Gilbert was also known as Allen and as Tremayne. He and his pilot were rescued by HMCS *St Laurent* after *Fidelity* was, presumed, sunk by U-boats in December 1942. 'JJ' was last heard of in the early 1960s when he visited Vancouver in command of the Guinean motor ship *Simandou*, where he contacted Province marine columnist Norman Hacking and explained that, during the war, he had been torpedoed in the North Atlantic and rescued by HMCS *St Laurent*.

39. Simon Artz was a famous department store on the waterfront at Port Said.

40. Socotra (now part of the Republic of Yemen) lies 250 miles east of the Horn of Africa, and the two islands to its south-west, in addition to their Arabic names, are known as The Brothers.

41. Noel William Bentley-Buckle, nicknamed 'Box' was born 26 December 1899 in Mallow, County Cork, Ireland. He was schooled in England and in 1919 left to visit an uncle in

Ceylon, stayed and became a rubber planter as well as rearing crocodile for their skins. After the rubber slump he turned his hand to tea, eventually owning a very successful tea plantation, *Dalhousie Estate* in *Maskeliya* in the hills above Colombo.

During the war he was Acting Lt Cdr, RNVR at HMS *Lanka* the RN base in Colombo. After the death of his first wife Mary, he married Dorothy Timms in 1948, the marriage was brief, they divorced and Box never married again. After leaving Ceylon in 1950 he settled in the Seychelles, where he continued his own business interests, owning the Pirates Arms Hotel on Mahé and several small schooners which transported cargo and passengers between the islands. He also had a lease on Remire Island (also known as *Eagle Island*) in the Amirantes, a group of outer Seychelles Islands, where he endeavored to harvest and export copra. He spent a brief period in Mombasa, returning to the Seychelles for his retirement, where he lived quietly on the island of Mahé until his death on 9 June 1974. He died of kidney failure, which the family believed was due to a reaction to the renal drugs he was being prescribed at the time. He is buried in a small private cemetery behind the police station overlooking Beau Vallon Beach, Mahé.

42. Moroni, the largest city of the Comoros islands and, since 1958, the capital.

43. James Leonard Brierley Smith (1897–1968) was a British-born South African ichthyologist. Before the war he identified a stuffed fish as a coelacanth, then known only as a fossil 65,000,000 years old. After the war he organised a search and in 1953 identified a second coelacanth.

44. Eric Hunt was owner and skipper of the schooner *Nduwaro* trading between Zanzibar, Madagascar and the Comoros. At Mutsamudu on the island of Anjouan on 21 December1952, fourteen years after the discovery of the first coelacanth, Hunt was approached by two fishermen and a schoolteacher, Affane Mohamed, with a fish which looked like the one pictured on the reward notices Hunt had posted. Hunt salted the fish and sailed to Mayotte, where he bought formalin from the director of medical services, and cabled Smith in South Africa. In 1956 Hunt disappeared after *Nduwaro* ran aground on the Geyser Bank between the Comoros and Madagascar.

45. A Lloyd's Open Form is a legal document used internationally to cover attempted marine salvage operations. It is 'open' because no price is set for the salvage, but is determined after the successful salvage under the law of England by an arbitrator. At the top of the form it says 'NO CURE – NO PAY' but the value of the ship and its cargo, and the dangers and difficulty in effecting the salvage, are taken into account by the arbitrator when making an award.

46. Richard David Shepherd CBE FRSA FGRA (1931–), British artist, famous for the wide skies of his paintings of wildlife in Africa.

47. Mukalla and Shibaam are ancient, towering cities in the historical region of the Arabian peninsula stretching eastwards from Yemen to the borders of Oman. The Hadrami diaspora has spread around the Indian Ocean and as far as Timor.

48. Major David Sheldrick (1919–77), Kenyan farmer and park warden, educated at Canford School, served in the Second World War in Abyssinia and Burma with the King's African Rifles, and at twenty-eight was the first warden of Tsavo National Park in Kenya.

49. The Six Day War was fought between 5 June and 10 June 1967 between Israel and its neighbouring states of Egypt, Jordan and Syria, beginning with a surprise air strike by Israel on Egypt, in which the Israelis seized the Gaza Strip and the Sinai Peninsula from Egypt, the West Bank and East Jerusalem from Jordan, and the Golan Heights from Syria.

50. The Edward Hotel in Durban is a world-famous hotel, built in 1911.

51. Lourenço Marques, now Maputo, is the capital and largest city of the former Portuguese colony of Mozambique. It is also known as the city of acacias, because of the trees along its avenues, and as the pearl of the Indian Ocean. Apart from fishing, chromite, coal, copra, cotton, hardwood, sugar and sisal are its chief exports and (in 2012) the city processes or manufactures aluminium, cement, furniture, pottery, rubber and shoes.

52. The Polana Hotel was built in 1922 on one of Lourenço Marques's acacia-lined avenues and was considered one of Africa's finest hotels.

53. J. T. Rennie & Co. were formerly Aberdeen-based shipowners on the London to Cape Town route, but in the 20th century a shipping agency in South Africa.

54. The Glorieuses or Glorioso Islands, officially the Archipel des Glorieuses, are in 2012 still a nature reserve, but with a meteorological station and garrisoned by the French Foreign Legion. They are claimed by Madagascar, the Seychelles and the Comoros.

55. EOKA or Ethniki Organosis Kyprion Agoniston or the National Organisation of Cypriot Fighters was a Greek Cypriot nationalist organisation which fought a violent campaign for self-rule and for union with Greece.

56. Makarios III (1913–77), archbishop and primate of the Cypriot Orthodox Church (1950–77), a leading advocate for union with Greece, and the first president of the republic of (southern) Cyprus (1960–77).

57. Sir James Richard Marie Mancham KBE (1939–) was the first president of Seychelles from 1976 to 1977. He founded the Seychelles Democratic Party and led it until 2005. Mancham encouraged tourism and promoted the building of an airport to make the Seychelles more accessible. Tourism increased and the economy developed and on independence Mancham won the popular vote when the British gave the Seychelles independence in 1976, but less than a year later he was deposed by France-Albert René, while he was attending the Commonwealth Heads of Government Conference in London.

58. *Anopheles* is a genus of mosquito, of which there are some 460 recognised types. Around a hundred types carry malaria or dengue fever.

59. Sir Bruce Greatbatch (1917–89), governor of Seychelles from 1969 to 1973, had the unpleasant duty of forcing the removal of the Chagos islanders from what would become the British Indian Ocean Territory in order to facilitate an American base on Diego Garcia.

60. France-Albert René (1935–), socialist president of Seychelles from 1977 to 2004, known as The Boss or Ti France.

61. Adnan Khashoggi (1935–), a Saudi Arabian socialite and businessman, sometimes accused of bribery in arms deals, and thought, in the 1980s, to be the richest man in the world.

62. Richard Luce (later Lord Luce KG, GCVO, PC, DL) (1936–) was elected MP in 1971 and was minister in the Foreign and Commonwealth Office 1979–82; he resigned over the failure of the FCO to predict or prevent the Falklands War.

INDEX